We All Begin in a Little Magazine

We All Begin in a Little Magazine
Arc and the Promise of Canada's Poets
1978–1998

edited by John Barton and Rita Donovan
Mike Feuerstack, Sharon Hawkins, Helen Humphreys
and Cheryl Sutherland

Arc Poetry Society

Carleton University Press

Ottawa, Canada

1998

Arc 40, Spring 1998

Arc: Canada's National Poetry Magazine, est. 1978.
Published by the Arc Poetry Society, est. 1996.

Co-editors: John Barton, Rita Donovan
Associate editors: Mike Feuerstack, Sharon Hawkins, Helen Humphreys, Cheryl Sutherland

The Arc Poetry Society gratefully acknowledges the support of the Canada Council, the Ontario Arts Council, the Regional Municipality of Ottawa-Carleton and our subscribers. *Arc* is published twice yearly in the Spring and Autumn. Manuscripts should be sent to our mailing address accompanied by a self-addressed, stamped envelope and a brief biographical note. Manuscripts without sase will not be returned. *Arc* is indexed by *Canadian Magazine Index* (also available online and on CD-ROM through *Canadian Business and Current Affairs*), *Canadian Periodical Index*, *Canadian Literary Periodicals Index*, and *Index of American Periodical Verse*. Arc is available on microfiche from Micromedia's Serials in Microforms program. *Arc* is distributed by the Canadian Magazine Publishers Association. Subscriptions cost $30 for 4 issues over 2 years. U.S. subscriptions: $40 CDN; sample issues Overseas: $50 CDN; Library subscriptions (Canadian, U.S., and overseas), at the same rates, are also available through Canebsco, Faxon, Faxon/SMS Canada and Readmore.

Back issues of *Arc* are available at $9.50 each (including postage and handling). Issues 1 to 10, which are out-of-print, are available on microfiche from Micromedia.

Send all manuscripts, correspondence, queries and subscription/back issue orders (accompanied by a cheque or money order made out to the Arc Poetry Society) to: *Arc*, Box 7368, Ottawa, Ontario, Canada K1L 8E4.

Copyright 1998 by the contributors.
All rights reserved.

Subject to copyright law; no part of this publication may be reproduced, stored in a retrieval system, or transmitted in any form or by any means, mechanical, photocopying, recording or ortherwise, without prior permission of the copyright holders. Please write c/o the Arc Poetry Society.

Canadian Cataloguing in Publication Data

Main entry under title:
    We all begin in a little magazine: Arc and the promise of Canada's poets, 1978-1998

Twentieth anniversary issue, no. 40, of Arc.
Co-published by Arc Poetry Society.
ISBN 0-88629-325-1

    1. Canadian poetry (English)-- 20th century. 2. Arc (Ottawa, Ont.). I. Barton, John, 1957-   II. Arc Poetry Society. III. Arc (Ottawa, Ont.)

PS8293.W4 1998   C811'.5408   C98-900538-0
PR9195.7.W4 1998

Front Cover: Regina Seiden, *Dora*, 1924. Oil on canvas, 76.9 x 66.7 cm. Collection, National Gallery of Canada, Ottawa. Reprinted with the permission of the Gallery. *Dora* is a portrait of the British-born, Montreal-raised poet, Elsa Gidlow, two of whose poems were included in *Arc* 31.

Design, layout, typesetting: Marie Tappin
Typeface: Caslon
Printer: Commercial Printers (Ottawa) Ltd
Cover printed on Cornwall paper, 10 point, coated one side, recycled; text on Plainfield Plus Smooth Brite White 140 M Text

for
Christopher Levenson
Michael Gnarowski and Tom Henighan
John Bell and Mark Frutkin
and Nadine McInnis

Table of Contents

Aspiration, Devotion and Community:
A Short Introduction
to the Long Life of a Little Magazine

With the publication of *We All Begin in a Little Magazine: Arc and the Promise of Canada's Poets, 1978-1998*, the editors celebrate *Arc*'s twentieth anniversary as one of Canada's only nationally distributed, poetry-exclusive literary journals. Founded in 1978 at Carleton University by Michael Gnarowski, Tom Henighan, and Christopher Levenson (who, after his two colleagues in the Department of English soon left the editorial board, continued as Editor until the magazine's tenth anniversary in 1988), *Arc* was part of a Canadian literary-magazine movement that rode the wave of the vibrant, sometimes profligate literary production unleashed after Canada's now legendary Centennial year. In the mid-to-late 1970s, many magazines were founded to document, shape, provide a forum and cultivate an audience for contemporary writing. After several issues, *Arc* left the umbrella of Carleton's financial support (though it continued to use the Department of English as its mailing address), receiving funding from various levels of government as well as the support of its subscribers, faithful and fickle alike. Associate editors came and went, as did editors. After Chris Levenson's resigned as editor in 1988 (he continued as an associate editor until 1990), this responsibly burdensome job was wisely split into two co-editorships that were held for a time by John Bell and Mark Fruitkin (1988–1990), then by Nadine McInnis and me (1990–1995), and now by Rita Donovan and me (1995 to the present). Without the volunteerism and support of many poets (and others) in the Ottawa literary community, *Arc* would have long ago gone the way of all flesh—or should I say the way of all lead type. Put it this way, without their help over the last two decades, we would not now be 'enjoying' the prospect of mounting of our own Web site.

In "We All Begin in a Little Magazine"[1] , the short story by Ottawa-born writer Norman Levine that lends its title to this anthology, an established, expatriate Canadian novelist rents the house of a London doctor for three weeks one summer. It turns out

---

1   Norman Levine's widely anthologized story, "We All Begin in a Little Magazine," was collected in his volume of short fiction, *Thin Ice*, published in 1979 by Deneau and Greenberg Publishers Ltd, of Ottawa.

that in his spare time Dr. Jones (the house's owner) publishes *ABC*, a small literary magazine whose potential contributors in his absence are constantly telephoning or dropping by the house at all hours to check on the status of their submissions, to seek advice and encouragement, or even to request a bed for the night. The chaos their interruptions create provokes the novelist to recall his own beginnings as a writer when, having arrived in England immediately after the Second World War, he and his colleagues were trying to get their first work published and have 'careers.' The little magazines like *ABC* (and *Arc*) of their apprenticeship were indispensable to the development of their sense of literary selfhood. "We used to send our stories, optimistically, to the *New Yorker* and the *Atlantic*. But that was like taking a ticket in a lottery. It was the little magazines who published us, who gave us encouragement and kept us going."

Any editor of a "little magazine" who reads Levine's story cannot fail to identify with the description of Dr. Jones's office: "The floor was cluttered with papers and magazines and manuscripts with letters and envelopes attached. On a wooden table, a large snap file had correspondence. A box had cheques for small amounts. There were also several pound notes, loose change, a sheet of stamps, and two packages of cigarettes.... There was typing paper, large envelopes, a typewriter, a phone, telephone directories, and some galleys hanging on a nail in the wall. A smaller table had an in-and-out tray to do with his medical work, more letters, and copies of the *Lancet*. The neatest part of the room was the area where unsold copies of *ABC* were on the floor against the far wall." Even today, with our dependence on computers, e-mail, and electronic artwork, this passage well illustrates how close to a cottage industry the business of literary publishing continues to be. For the editors of any literary journal, it is a constant, sometimes solitary, often anonymous act of devotion involving not only the fine details of style and craft, but the tedium of production schedules, monitoring renewal rates and paying invoices (though in Canada, at the behest of increasingly more insecure granting agencies, the management of a literary magazine is an exhausting act of accountability that has less to with literature and more to do with pleasureless appeasement).

However, to subscribers or the casual newsstand browsers, the mechanics of editing, production and financial management are invisible and secondary. Any literary magazine is emphatically about the new work of the authors it publishes and the recent books it reviews. In *We All Begin in a Little Magazine*, readers will rediscover poems that appeared in *Arc* over the last twenty years by some of Canada's best writers who began and often continue to publish in *Arc* or in its peers. These poems show their authors to advantage at various stages in their careers, sometimes at an early brush with publication, or later, in their full maturity, or, more likely, somewhere in between. Their combined presence in *Arc*, and now in *We All Begin in a Little Magazine*, suggests how the promise illustrated early on in a poet's writing life evolves toward the confidence earned through years of commitment (in other words, the promise kept) to his or her craft.

Levine's narrator recalls the sense of community that the little magazines fostered, and how the little bits of money paid to contributors like himself for a poem, a book review or a short story momentarily helped make ends meet, covering a meal or two or perhaps paying for a package of cigarettes. It is unarguably a nostalgic view of the down-and-out life of the novice, but it is difficult to dismiss Levine's description of the satisfactions of publication itself. Like the hackneyed cigarette smoked after sex, publication was almost as good as (and sometimes better than) the act of writing itself. And like all other impulsive acts, making one's deathless *bons mots* publicly available in editions of 200 or 300 copies had unanticipated, long-term effects: "I had complete faith then in those little magazines. What I didn't know was that what they bred was infectious. They infected a lot of young people with the notion that to be involved with literature was somehow to be involved with the good life. And by the time you learned differently, it was usually too late."

The faith, whether ill-advised or not, that Norman Levine celebrates in his short story goes both ways, for the editors of small magazines like *Arc* also become "infected" by the unshakeable, idealistic belief that what their contributors have to say and how they say it (not to mention the act of publishing itself) matters and is even *ennobling.* On good days, most editors believe that by publishing what authors and readers alike might later view to be juvenalia, a work-in-progress or, worse, a candidate for burning, they can, in some small way, help nurture a national literature. Poor dears, we won't break the bad news to them, will we?

The current editors of *Arc* would argue that the poets represented in this anthology have become or are in the process of becoming significant voices in Canadian writing. At the very least they have collectively been active in the national literary scene over the last twenty years. Certainly they are important to the history of *Arc*. On that count alone, we thank them for their continued support by making their work available to us for publication. That the magazine's changing corps of editors and associate editors have had the opportunity since 1978 to "encourage" such poets and to "keep [them] going" is as it should be and is without doubt our most important reason to exist. Consequently, we are in complete empathy with Norman Levine's short story, even if its narrator was eventually driven to complete distraction by the endless parade of Dr. Jones's and *ABC*'s literary hopefuls and proteges. By the time his three-week holiday was over, he was more than glad to vacate the selfless doctor's house in favour of the relative quiet of the sea-side resort town he calls home. So much for the good life he dreamed of in his youth...

That all said, and despite the sometimes soul-destroying work, there is nothing more satisfying for an editor than to take delivery of the latest issue or for a contributor to discover a copy of it—with his or her poem printed *correctly* inside—waiting one day in the mail. After forty issues and twenty years in print, the editors of and contributors to *Arc* can only hope that our readers past, present and future have felt, do, and will continue to feel exactly the same.

John Barton
May 1998

Ceremony for Ancestors

Carol Shields

Getting Born

Odd how no one knows how
    it feels to be born,
    whether it's one smooth watery ride
    down green ether-muffled air
    or whether the first breath burns
    in the lungs with the redness of flames

Only the time and place are fixed
    Chicago Illinois 1935
in the midst of the depression as folks said
    then.   The hospital still stands
    a pyramid of red bricks
    made clumsy by airshafts   only now
    there's a modern wing
    smooth as an office tower
The doctor is dead

The doctor is dead
    not only dead but erased
    "What was his name anyway? An Irish name
    began with an M."   There's something
    careless about this forgetting
He died in the war
    probably   a young man with
    smooth hands, a blank face

The doctor is dead
    Birth is a procedure
    Coming alive
    is only half a ceremony

All we need is breath
    a clutching at simple air
    a feeble absence

You slipped out like a lump of butter
    my mother said

The End of the War

There was our mother
on the back porch
waving a meatfork
and crying out the words
Unconditional Surrender

It happened to be suppertime
when the news came purling
out of the old Philco and
setting her on fire

She forgot to take off her apron
even   it was the tired
end of a hot day   and a wonder
to see her step and lurch
like a crazy woman

If only we'd taken a picture
and put it in a frame—
our mother   dancing across the porch
with her single flashing weapon
uniquely in hand
crying victory victory   and hurling
us into the future

Kenneth Sherman

Fedora

On a downtown street corner
near Tip Top Tailors
I find myself
looking for my father.

I pass a darkened hat shop
south on Spadina
that displays a fedora—
the sort he used to wear

in the dead heart of winter
when he'd come home from work
drained, without words.
In the sudden warmth of the house

his glasses fog.
He takes off his coat and his hat
then pours himself
a thimble of Scotch.

Under the bald glare
of a suburban streetlight
our driveway is filling
with snow.

My father eats his late supper
then again puts on
his hat and his coat.
My pillow is next

to my bedroom window
so I can hear
the clear and solitary
scrape of his shovel.

The sound slices through me.
What is he shovelling
if not the days
that lie buried

in the banks of whiteness
that will melt
or be carried by wind?
On a closet shelf,

years later, I find
my father's fedora
with its stained sweatband,
the possibility of its soft folds,

its rigid brim.
When I run my hand inside
along the cool satin lining
I can feel the absence.

Somewhere, my father is travelling
with what he could not give.
What he gave
I hold now in my hand.

Anne Szumigalski

Summer 1928

almost asleep Charles hears his mother say to her friend
Uncle Norman I don't care what you're wearing I don't
care what you've been eating just come over here and sit
down beside me at the piano   in bed the child is telling
himself the story of everything that has happened, of the
man sitting beside his mother playing and singing *To Althea
from Prison* which the boy interprets as the tale of the heart's
refusal he falls into a dream of wisteria a bower outside a
tavern in Italy where anything grows claims his mother but
here in this beastly climate it's hard to find a flowering
creeper though there are climbing shrubs enough to cover
any balcony with a thicket of tender leaves where linnets
nest and sing

the boy sees himself in the attic fondling the trailing
teagown his aunt is said to have put away for ever when
word came that her lover had been picked off by a sniper
Charles lifts it out of its squashed cardboard box and
slips it over his head the chiffon is a turbid green like
ditchwater for a moment the gown hangs silkily on his
naked shoulders then with a whisper falls apart and floats
to the floor each piece no bigger than an envelope he gathers
them up and folds them back into the blue tissue assuring
himself that after a year the garment will heal and become
whole and beautiful again he has only to be patient and wait
the twelvemonth through

from downstairs the sound of the two voices the four hands
trails away to silence the child makes himself think of
those twenty fingers resting on the piano keys he would
like to be another person a boy his own age but with different
coloured eyes and hair lying on the bottom of the sea looking
up through grey water at the metal hull of a ship passing
overhead   in the first class ballroom two golden-haired
women have just finished playing a duet on the piano
the last trickle of sound dribbles out into the ocean
the strange boy puts out a languid hand and catches the
music in the guise of undulating seaweed

Charles darling his mother has said it more than once
your uncle Norman is the owner of an excellent baritone
when she says *Charles darling* he's always startled because
that's how she speaks to his father the first Charles who
perhaps has returned and is standing behind him in his
majesty's uniform the tropical one because he's just
arrived from a redhot place where mangos grow on a tall
tree a man in a turban shakes the tree and when the fruit
falls he makes it into chutney which the officers eat from
dishes like pink porcelain blossoms while the brown soldiers
sit on blankets spread over the dead grass and are served
nothing but hard round cakes of rivermud arranged in neat
rows on old tin trays rusting a little at the rims

it's afternoon and nurse is pinning a terry square on one
of the twins who are the result she says candidly of his
father's last leave or maybe that Mr Norman but no she
laughs darkly he'd rather be godfather to many than father
to one he's not such a bad sort for doesn't he take the twins
off our hands most afternoons and give us all a rest from
their squalling

the man whom the boy hates picks up the babies one under
each arm and dumps them into the perambulator   as he
starts off it begins to rain pittering on the pramhoods
but that doesn't bother Uncle who strides away up the village
singing his loudest Nurse and Charles watch him go until
they can't hear the singing and crying any more then she
goes upstairs to tidy and he picks up the book he's decided
to read about fighter aircraft not that he cares much for it
but it makes him feel more like some of the boys he goes
to school with

Norman is back the babies are asleep in their soft white shawls
smelling of their mother's sandalwood soap she's in a silly
mood and comes giggling out of the drawing room inviting the
man to stay as though he was a stranger she was meeting
for the first time it's tea and cake in the summer house
Charles is not included he has his in the kitchen with Nurse
when he turns his head and looks through the kitchen
window he can see the creepers growing up the side of
the summerhouse where rain is still dripping from the
eaves a large drop is hanging from the lip of one of
the greenish cobea blossoms he can't make up his mind
whether it will trickle down the striped purple throat
of the flower or whether it will fall outwards onto the
leaves which are withering and turning pink with autumn

a storm comes at night and Charles gets up trembling
wanting to get into bed with Nurse who is not afraid of
anything he knows her back turned towards him in sleep
will smell reassuringly of buttered bread on the turn of
the stair he sees his mother with Uncle Norman their hands
are clasped tightly but she is holding the man away from
her by the length of her white freckled arms thunder breaks
the air then hush a very faint word comes from between her
lips what's she saying what's she saying?

the next streak of lightning lifts her hair it stands up
all around her head like a brilliant foxfur halo little
white tongues of flame flash from the curled ends of her
red hair

Uncle Norman whimpers and lets go and she sinks down onto
the stairs moaning or crying or laughing it's difficult
to tell which   Charles decides she is laughing and goes
back to bed to dream of italy where they stayed in a room
above a courtyard *so long* Father says buckling on his sam
browne looking into his son's eyes for a long time

then he picks up his cap and swaggerstick from the chair
by the brass bed where his wife is lying with the quilt
pulled up over her face refusing to look refusing to
say goodbye

Don McKay

Lost Sisters

so small
I can't pick you up in my arms or on
the radar of imagination, in my dreams you are
the ghosts of ghosts.
Your names
fit loosely and you slide
between the letters, too fine
for this ordinary mesh.
Uncontaminated as a tribe known
only to itself, you can't
be spoken to or looked at, perish
when you hit the page.

What's it like, up there?
Do you ache for earth the way we ache for air, do you dream
in loam and humus?
Are you bored with your nunnery,
its pale symmetries and soft
pre-raphaelite decor?
Do you read fairy tales of Burger Kings and Dairy Queens,
aristocrats of the banal?

No traces of you in the attic—
no snapshots, footprints, spoon-marks on the table
where you never beat the rhythm of those appetites
you never had—your absence like abandoned
Ariadne's thread insinuating
everywhere, the ripcord,
the sad clause in the fine print,
the catch,
my lost sisters,
this tiny catch in my voice.

David Zieroth

Here the Waiting Begins

Father drives
the tractor whining by in second
and the stone-boat drags
over the furrows of soil soft as black
and the flat patterns cross the field,
three sons follow, toss back roots, stones,
bones

the sun turns to
                    jet plane
two men, a cockpit, so
perfectly stiff and still and
shaking the ground with its letters: RCAF
—the dogs howling, running away from their tails—
so low and silver and
I thought I could see the rivets then
the helmeted men
just above trees

and áll my brothers
standing still in the black fields
arms loose as clubs
waiting for the dogs
watching the sky
waiting for the silver stone

Susan Glickman

Oranges

I

My friend's small daughter cries
and we call it hunger
and give her an orange.

She takes in her two hands, peers into
this globe, this mirror of the sun,
bronze heart of an idol

and her strong fingers press its pitted skin
and stroke out such perfume
that we all know hunger
and name it "orange".

II

On the road to Mycenae in the dog-days in June
    what glitter, what lanterns set in green
        abundance of orange-groves
heavy by roadside, untended
    open to any hand. And passing
        we pluck the offered fruit, a mystery
            old as these walls. Precious
            as Agamemnon's crown.

III

Sometimes when you're walking down the street
and it's raining, say, and your collar's up, you shrink
inside your skin, see nothing, don't care to. And then
you stop for a red light and on the corner is an old woman
bent over her bags with a look of such radiance
you believe she has the answer to everything in there
with the oranges and the carton of milk. She is the mother
you lost before you were born, you wake out of your life
into your life, there by the mailbox, under the umbrellas.
She turns the corner, shuffling her feet, her bent back
black as all the others, you lose her in the crowd,
you walk on. What were you thinking before, mathematics
of loss. The day
has been given you to start over, and you do.

IV

My grandfather could skin an orange
in one elaborate loop, a snake-skin shed
recoiled to mimic fruit

My grandmother made roses out of radish,
too dainty to eat,
and tomato crowns, edged in jagged red;

And when I serve my friends
I too build garden, castle,
the land of heart's desire.

Hunger's a name for what we want, not need.
The simplest thing's
more than sufficient—an orange
the deepening wash of sunset, field of poppies
such perilous excess.

Michael Crummey

Ski Hill

On a clear day you could see the entire town from there,
the rows of company houses and backyard fences,
the Union Hall, the community pool,
the cottage hospital where my mother worked
off and on for fifteen years;
three church spires, two small schools,
the ballfield where my father slipped and broke his leg
in a rundown between third and home before I was born

Down the hill's back slope the grey remains of a wooden ski run
closed long before my parents married
by lack of snow and the cost of keeping it running,
unrecognizable as anything now but the scar of something human
almost buried in shrubs and moss and blueberry bushes
and beyond that the worthless sprawling beauty
of the barrens

The scrawl of mills to the south-east
smokey-grey buildings stained yellow with sulphur,
around them the train sheds and core-shacks
the huge red warehouse where they laid ice
every winter before the arena was built
and housed almost the entire population on Saturday nights
when the Corner Brook Royals came to town

The white staff office out front, a sign proclaiming
ASARCO: TRESPASSERS WILL BE PROSECUTED;
the double line of railway tracks that marked
the border of company property
where strikers stood every four years
with placards and cigarettes, occasionally
burning a train caboose to the wheels
upending a management car that had
tried to cross the picket line

Out of sight behind the mills are the *Glory Holes*
excavations the size of small lakes,
and underneath it all the tangle of shafts
where men worked eight hours a shift
drilling the darkness for zinc and copper,
eating a daily sandwich lunch
My mother watched them come in at regular intervals
cursing ugly cuts or sprains
or just the pain   the goddamn pain
of a limb suddenly missing or maimed
by their machines or blind rock or a long fall in the dark
And once every three years or so,
a man she would know by name
wheeled in beneath the white silence of a sheet

At the far edge of town the three grave-yards placed side by side
a triptych of fenced cemeteries, most of the plots overgrown now
with shrubs and weeds grazing high as the rowed headstones,
tree roots cracking rectangles of concrete
Homes standing empty, doorways and window frames
turning grey with the weather,
a few people left to small pensions and welfare
and to memories like these,
the scar of something human that's had its season
something I've never known as intimately
or seen as clear as I did those early summer afternoons
watching it from the bare skull of Ski Hill

Penn Kemp

from **Other/Mother**

mother I take your hand
and thank you whom I
so long resisted
running backward in panic
to be more, other, than
a mother

I who so long fought
against you, against life
to maintain a separate
space which tho stillborn
was my own and safe

I who never dared look
direct, who danced askance
from that anxious image,
twisting to cut the knot

now look you in the face
and live

your fire does not sear,
the children no longer
fear stepping into stream
to be enlivened

I wash off our masks and
laugh as you laugh, dance
in your footsteps and on,
fanning all our aspects out
moving into wholeness

thru the door of generation,
my thought is my body—

this is a woman speaking, no—
this is a woman as she is
speaking

David Henderson

Woman with Suitcase

My brother and I huddle at the top
of the patio stairs, two small animals
who thought the sky was safe,
charred stiff by sudden lightning.

Father stands apart, taut, ever-silent,
pouched eyes watching you stride away
with your fine leather suitcase
along the sea-bordering meadow.

You thread a determined path
through the cows you've always feared;
they lift their heads, belling your departure
till you disappear around the dog-leg.

Late that evening, you return, unbowed,
lips set. The local fishermen, too,
sail out with the morning mist, return
as the mountains slip the sun behind them.

Who knows in what uncharted depths
their nets have swelled, what myopic creatures
they've brought up, what thoughts
have come and gone with passing waves?

Nothing is ever said, and we make-believe
it never happened. Soon, the dread that coiled
around us when you walked away unwinds
to reveal something unexpected, and I'm sorry,

but it wasn't the thought of you leaving
that struck us mute, but the taut, silent shadow
Father cast as he stared narrowly ahead,
his certainties driven rigid through his soul.

Robert Hilles

Boy in a Choir

It's not murder that brings him to this church. He wants to feel god's affection while standing on a wooden bench. Sometimes god is late too not arriving until the choir is nearly finished practicing for the day. Late or not god is welcomed. The boy can see that god has stopped being holy years ago that he listens to the conversations of sinners because he is more interested in gossip than in salvation. Still he remains loyal to those he has abandoned. Even his clothes reflect neglect: his shoes worn through. The boy has heard lovers tip toe from his mother's room at night and each of them walks like a god, the slow and natural walk of a man satisfied in love. Leaving the choir practice each Sunday, the boy pauses near the grave of his father. He listens for a sound any sound but all he ever hears is the music of the children in the nearby playground. Still their music is so beautiful he wants to dance in someone's arms. The boy is not disappointed that god can bring little more than sleep to our lives. But when the boy sings in the church beside other boys and girls he can feel his mother's arms around her lover slowly slacken can see her turn to look out a window at the Sunday traffic. Nearly on tip toes the boy reaches for the highest note in a hymn and as he does god slips out the side entrance and heads for the boy's house.

John Barton

When I Was Fifteen

The land was flat then,
inarticulate,
the horizons mute.
No trees stood against the sky,
only highrises
thick with shadow.

When I was at school
my mother worked until late evening.
At four I bussed home to the suburbs,
did my lessons.
I ate supper alone.

At night TV on,
my heart felt the rhythm of ship on ocean.
In my dreams Atlantis loomed,
its cliffs sharp against the dusk.
Mountains thrust up in the distance
as I heaved closer to shore.

In the morning
I woke to the odour of sea salt
rising hot and damp
from my bedclothes.

Tim Bowling

Sturgeon

I

We believe them ancient, prehistoric,
their strangely-whiskered, small-eyed faces
like those of Oriental villains
in silent movies, floating up
from currents of opium to sell
sweet girls into slavery;
we believe them alien, mysterious,
royals of a remote dynasty
reigning over the muddied depths,
at bliss in a bubbling dream.

We believe because
we seek some distance
from their power, the gaze
that mocks our blood's short course:
seventy years! the bones
poke through our skin like sandbars
at the lowering tide;
we can't love long enough
to penetrate their thick, drugged world,
that haze of silt
falling in the riverbottom's eerie light
like dust in a streetlamp's glow:
we fear their exotic ugliness
for in it shines
the commonplace beauty of loss.

II

One autumn night in the early seventies
at the mouth of the Fraser River
800 pounds of history woke
from its long, blind sleep
to wear my father's finest meshes
across its eyes
like a bridal veil
and jilted a dozen other men
before it slept at last
the century in a nylon coffin
gasping at the nearness of the stars:
roped to the stern, dragged against
the rushing tide till drowned,
the years left a dark swath
in the dark waters:
"Winched on the wharf," my father said
quiet over his morning coffee
as I delayed my walk to school,
"it looked like a beam of moonlight."

III

Most often now, they're young,
three pounds or four,
just past being a delicacy
on the tongues of the rich:
imagine a child's living eyes
in the face of a dead man,
imagine history condensed to seconds
hung like lizards in the drifting air:

pulled from the net, in our hands
they twist for freedom; are we
an exotic ugliness they have come
to fear? Can our gaze reflect
a loss beyond our own?
Released, their tiny bellies
flash pale in the green tide,
shards of an old moonlight
destined never to stir
the silts of the kingdom.

IV

My father at seventy
still remembers
the great sturgeon
tall in the chill air
as a tower of bone:
"I couldn't believe,"
he often says
"how something so white
could cast such a dark shadow."

And we stare into the river
one man
waiting for the black
to lift from the earth,
brushing, with a single thought,
the soot from our trailing selves.

Barbara Folkart

tear water pooling

it has been a song, each time,
Schubert coming from the next room,
simple as water,
or Benjamin Britten,
and I have sat down in the hallway,
my sports bag on the floor beside me
my swim gear ready to go

and I have wept

*

what spells me
when I swim the butterfly
is the instant of arcing
out and skimming over
before the plunge back in,
the fraction of flight that costs you
everything you have in your arms,
leaves you shaking at the end of the lane—

the gasp, the plunge from blue to bright to blue

*

it's the elusive elements I seek,
the bright the blue
air and water—

cool fugitive fluids

*

flying wrings warmth from water
wrests heart out of air—
my flesh and thirst
the warmth and tingle in my muscles

a kind of love

*

mother-water
to flow with fight with
cool embrace that pleasures
safeties frees me
glistens me surging
out and arching in

curve of out and in
escape and snug

the spool unreeled then wound back in

*

now it's my mother that's escaping
played out
unreeling into air

no way to wind her back

*

water and air cooling
nothing left there
but the longing,
endless ripple,
no way now

to ever get it right

*

the song's as simple as that,
simple as water with its heart unlocked
would be—

the song is where the tears have pooled

Mary di Michele

from **Crown of Roses**

I think that someone will remember us in another time.

                     Sappho trans. Jim Powell

*

My daughter: like yours, with yellow hair,
forsythia, broom in bloom, jonquil, crocus,
daffodil and narcissus, her headband
        crocheted lace

she bought for herself at the Gap
because I couldn't find one to match—
because even laurel could only be
        eclipsed by her curls,

this morning freshly shampooed
and smelling of apple pectin.

*

Don't you know your dress thrills the men
but me more. I don't care
                if you ever take it off!
The way your gown, its soft linen cloth
                    clings to your hips
with the smoothness of marble
           but oh, warm to the touch.

The colour becomes you,
           shade of hyacinth
crushed underfoot, their fragrant bleeding
or hue of grape
        foaming in Orpheus's cup...

The virgin is inviolate
        the bride must wear violet.

*

Why is it always Aphrodite's fault?
                          Who is really to blame
that I wasted my words (so they said)
                          describing fashion,
but tell me how could I, without numbing the senses,
                          forget to mention
her sandals were gold lamé
                    and braided at the back!

*

The moon is half
                full (or half.
gone) the moon is round,
                  stone ground, a peasant loaf
sweetened with golden corn,
                  mealy and moist,

a peasant loaf when divided, when devoured
                          at the feast for which
you arrive too late.

Hunger makes even crumbs glow
                          as brilliantly as wishing
stars. In the dark the moon
dazzles more than the sun
                          (for which we feel less
need)

all night long Sappho
              I also sleep alone...

Di Brandt

A Small Earth Trilogy
for H.D.

1

coming to greet you in the corridor
the lost golden boys with their wounds
the whiff of an old choir-song your
mother & her sisters dancing round
the golden calf *drede Heljedag* not
caring a fig about Moses & his wrath
yes & with Grandma in cahoots you
& your sisters posed as Muses for the
camera on the beach Jesus listening
to country music with his beard shaved
off Mary mother Mary when will my
true lord come i'm lost i'm oh so lonely
languishing in shade dreaming empty
hieroglyphs on empty walls Helen
shimmering phantom-like Egyptian
the sea-enchanted the gold-burning
sands

2

finding another beside me in the dying
world unexpectedly proffering love i ask
Jesus i ask Isis give us this day a future
to hold in our hands a pearl a bead a comb
a cup of bowl glinting half-hidden in the
sand Aganetha Justina Maria hiding your
laughter in the barn give me more give me
more than stones i want red raspberries
& wild roses blooming in the snow the
shoes of dancing princesses spilling the
inkwell & the Sen Sen & the Word the cow
kicking over the milking stool all the cats
saved Mary Nettie Sarah Leina Jessie &
Annie *the holy ghost* shaking your red gold
brown hair perfumed against the sun your
secret fire your flaming desire

chant the words slowly on your tongue
trace the Egyptian lines on your face
once again with your hand now is the
time of grace now is the time of harvest
squeeze the purple fruit rudely into your
mouth dribble it down your chin all that
must die can now be reborn Rosie Rosie
Ring arounda Rosie *aurora borealis* every
ransomed daughter a jewelled princess
yo! let the rivers flow let the prairie
grass grow let the wild rice sow its old
magic in the wind let the God shaped
papyrus shaped hole in our hearts disappear
the great styrofoam wound in the sky
weeping be healed

April Bulmer

Woman With the Flow of Blood

I offered turtledoves and pigeons; healers and midwives a
heavy sack of coins. Still the old snake shed her red skins.
Her woman cloth. At night, she dragged her long belly
through my tent and into the dry thighs of the desert. In
dreams Jesus beat across the sand as a raven, taking the snake
limp in his beak; snagged his soft wings in a tree. But in the
morning my body was a weak basket where the blood coiled.
And the men did not play their pipes for me.

Twelve years I bled. My spirit so weak, but still the dreams
flew.

The day Jesus crossed over the sea, I went to him in the crowd
and I did reach out and touch a tassel that hung from his gar-
ment. The snake opened her wide jaw and pulled her thick
tail into herself: my womb was firm and healthy as an apple.

And he praised the tight knot of my faith: the dreams that
did not crawl away from my heart, nor slough my body.

Pat Jasper

On Rereading *War and Peace* Twenty-Three Years Later

*A name read long ago in a book contains
within its syllables the strong wind
and brilliant sunshine that prevailed
while we were reading it*

                        Marcel Proust

The summer we were twenty
he worked nights on an oil rig
and I, pregnant with our first child,
would stay up—reading and waiting.

A succession of hot, muggy nights,
the only escape to burrow into
the snows of 1812, the chill and thaw
of equivocal love affairs. That
and cold wet towels plastered
over my swollen body.

Sometimes the men worked double shifts.
I never knew if or when he'd be home.
Two roustabouts were killed that summer,
several lost fingers and toes. Each
leave-taking was fraught with finality,
each homecoming, a gift.

I would pry the lunchbox from his fingers,
grateful he still had five, make him
strip on the back porch, the overalls
so stiff with mud and grease, they'd stand
by themselves. He'd nod off in the tub
while I scrubbed him white again
with pumice, filling him in on
the latest comings and goings
of Andrey, Natasha and Pierre.
He'd ask sleepy questions
about Nikolay, his favourite,
oblivious of what fate had in store.

When the sun came up, we'd pull
the shades and crawl between
clean sheets, cool and white
as snow, our Russian ghosts lingering
restive above the covers, so close
you could see their breath
in the morning air.

Jill Battson

Yvette, Yvonne

Memoria

Joined at the skull
we spend our life
looking at the breasts of the sister
our mother and god
raised us in a circus
we loved the pin heads
because they have their own

       as Yvette I love eating
       as Yvonne I put on weight

In South Central
we reach out to
people who cross the road
when we walk crablike towards them
we are both
a pain in the neck

       as Yvette I am quiet
       as Yvonne I am gregarious

Cold metal printer's dream:
we have learned to read the newspaper
upside down
to snoop at the sister's journal entry
upside down

       as Yvette I drink coffee
       as Yvonne I can't sleep

We can never pull
a sweater over our head
a hairbrush over our skull
a lone shower off
we can be lonely
but never alone

      as Yvette I stay up 'til one
      as Yvonne I'm tired in the mornings

As tradition
we are gospel singers
god gave us our voice
to raise thanks
with gospel words
melodies in red gowns
tinting our skin

      I can't sleep when you watch TV
      I watch TV to hear god's call.

Patricia Young

Weird Genes

Aunt Rebecca's daughters, eight years apart,
all walked in their sleep like their father.
She said my oldest cousin began
her journey into the dark at three years old.
Ran the bath full of cold water, took off
her nightgown, returned naked to bed.
The next one with wild red hair was regular as clockwork.
A winter night when she opened all the windows,
the front and back doors, set the table with her mother's best china.
At four the youngest girl sat at the edge
of her bed and expertly laced up her skates though
my aunt said she couldn't do this for herself
at the rink on Saturday afternoons.
She stumbled through the house, blades cutting into
hardwood floors, dreaming ice, dreaming popcorn, dreaming
figure-eights. Once my aunt woke to my uncle
standing on a chair at 3 a.m., flashlight in hand,
peering out a window boarded up years before.
She confessed to my mother it drove her mad.
Years of sticking bone-handled knives
between the jamb and their bedroom doors
to keep them in. A lifetime of waking up
to furniture rearranged, lampshades in the garden,
the fridge emptied, her false teeth on the back porch.
Said it was a good thing her husband's brothers never married,
a blessing their weird genes were contained
on a small sheep farm in Northern Wales.
A chill going up her spine Aunt Rebecca imagines
those four bachelors wandering the mountains
of Snowdonia: wide-eyed, in night caps,
bereft of their musical tongues.

Nadine McInnis

Reliquary

Crosses are vanishing
from above doorways and beds.
Instead, each of us lives
with a humming vault in our kitchens
the size of our own coffin,
its perpetual drone
like the ringing in the ears
of explorers before they freeze
or go mad.

This is a tall icy country
either in total darkness
or total light
with no line possible between.
Children put eyes to the slit,
pull slowly
to catch light snapping on.
Never are they thin or fast
enough

and the few who crawl inside
hurtle into their past
are found curled, blue chicks
feathered with frost, in eggs
that will never hatch,
and only melons
withering in the crisper
remember how they got there.

We were warned about this
even before kidnappers,
yet our crayon suns and flower bursts
were drawn to its magnetic pole.
Like mothers before me
I tape her feverish colours onto white,
a shrine to her quick vision,
a prayer that cold also preserves.

Anne Szumigalski

Jesus

A child sees Jesus coming towards her through the glass of the nursery door. When his reflection fades she turns around and there he is standing right behind her. She knows him by his beard, by his pierced hands, by his bare feet cold on the linoleum. He bends down to kiss her, and she notices that his halo stays there on the wall above him empty, waiting for his head to fit back in.

She's pleased with the visitation, of course, but she'd much rather he'd sent an angel with long feathered wings to lift her up and fly with her over the tops of trees, over oceans full of rocky islands with seabirds nesting on them.

Her mother has warned her that Jesus is simply a man, with all the things a man has: bristly chin, hairy knees, bony feet, this and that. *Sooner or later*, her mother has said, *he will come for you and take you on a long journey*.

The child glances outside, and sure enough there is a very old donkey with downtrodden hooves tethered in the garden. The scruffy-looking thing is chewing on some lilies in the perennial border. Spotted orange petals and blacktipped stamens are scattered about on the grass.

Jesus has his arm around her now and is urging her through the door and down the path towards the back gate. Panic, like a longnecked bird, is opening and closing its beak in her throat. Nothing comes out, not even the crumbly hiss of a murrh.

She looks back at the house, at the nursery door still standing a little open. *I should go back and shut it*, she says to the man who is squeezing her shoulder with large possessive fingers. He doesn't answer but points with his other hand towards the road where she sees her mother getting into her small yellow car. She has on her big straw hat, the one she wears for picnics. Her father is already sitting in the passenger seat. He has taken off his glasses and is breathing on them, first one side then the other. Just as the car moves off, he holds them up to the light and begins polishing the lenses with his large white pocket handkerchief.

Heather Spears

Hind, Eating Fish in Denmark

Hind with her long red nail
peels out the eye of the herring
(smoked the colour of lead or leather
flattened like the bog bodies
found under fake hills
in this northern land of her exile)

peels it out, eats it
while I protest and say
something vague about
poisonous concentrations of Vitamin A
imagining (behind the print
of articles that I forget)
more north, Greenland, the gutted seal
or yellowish bear dead on the snow
the polar liver, the extreme eye—

then I remember the island, the dog's plate
where I dumped codfish cooked with rye
bread, and, inside the courtyard
halfdoor, safe from their marauding,
whole fish-heads for the cats, cooling on yesterday's news.

Later, going in with a broom,
I'd sweep up jaws more brittle than a bird's,
tiny concave saucers that had held a cheek of meat,
crescents of gills, and knitting needle bones
chewed clean even of their smell,
deserted by the flies.

But, there would be an eye—!
skidding under the broom-edge, berry white,
another one - no nick, no pupil, nothing to hold it by.
The dogs, too, nosed them high and dry
in their slicked dish. Animals know,
just like the Esquimaux.

Hind, daintily eating between white teeth,
laughs at me. Her Iraqi name
means India. Don't, Hind, it will grow
out of your forehead, first a sear
small as the end of a cigarette, then a swollen scar
long and almond, with lashes painted on.
It will wink at us and stare.

Stephen Heighton

Ceremony for Ancestors: Kōya San

They said *Burn with an inside flame*
like Japanese lanterns
we would see each other clearly

     Burn away the fingered ribs containing
a flammable heart, burn away
the wrinkled tissue, we would see this much, at least,
of our flesh and family—

          "I recognize you,"
a stranger said. "I think I do. Your father's
living image. I suppose
he must be here
tonight?"
       I told him no.
          Tonight
candelabra of children amble
among stars, follow the trails of flame
calling parents
and calling them, calling them
to suppers by the tomb, by candle, they said
Burn
Burn away
that part of us our children, even
could not have seen
          Burn what they might discover
          Burn what they might infer: flames' real tints

the urn in ribs that felt
that death we held inside us—-

                        They told me, "Look

with the eye's wick ignited
into forest behind the tombs
up the bird-encircled mountain
Look
your mother is that gravid darkness
urging you to burn"

                I did not answer—-
we are the living, we must suffer
the obscure vigils of the dead—-

and eyes pressing from the forest,
voices at the river's source catch flame
in the world's cold furnace

                    Burn

Mother, Father, you cindering root-
fuse of my flesh and hours, you too are foreign
ghosts, and I am
haunted by your absence.

                        Japanese lanterns along a bridge
drift in the water reflections
like the moon, repeated, years in a mirror
a face you do not know.

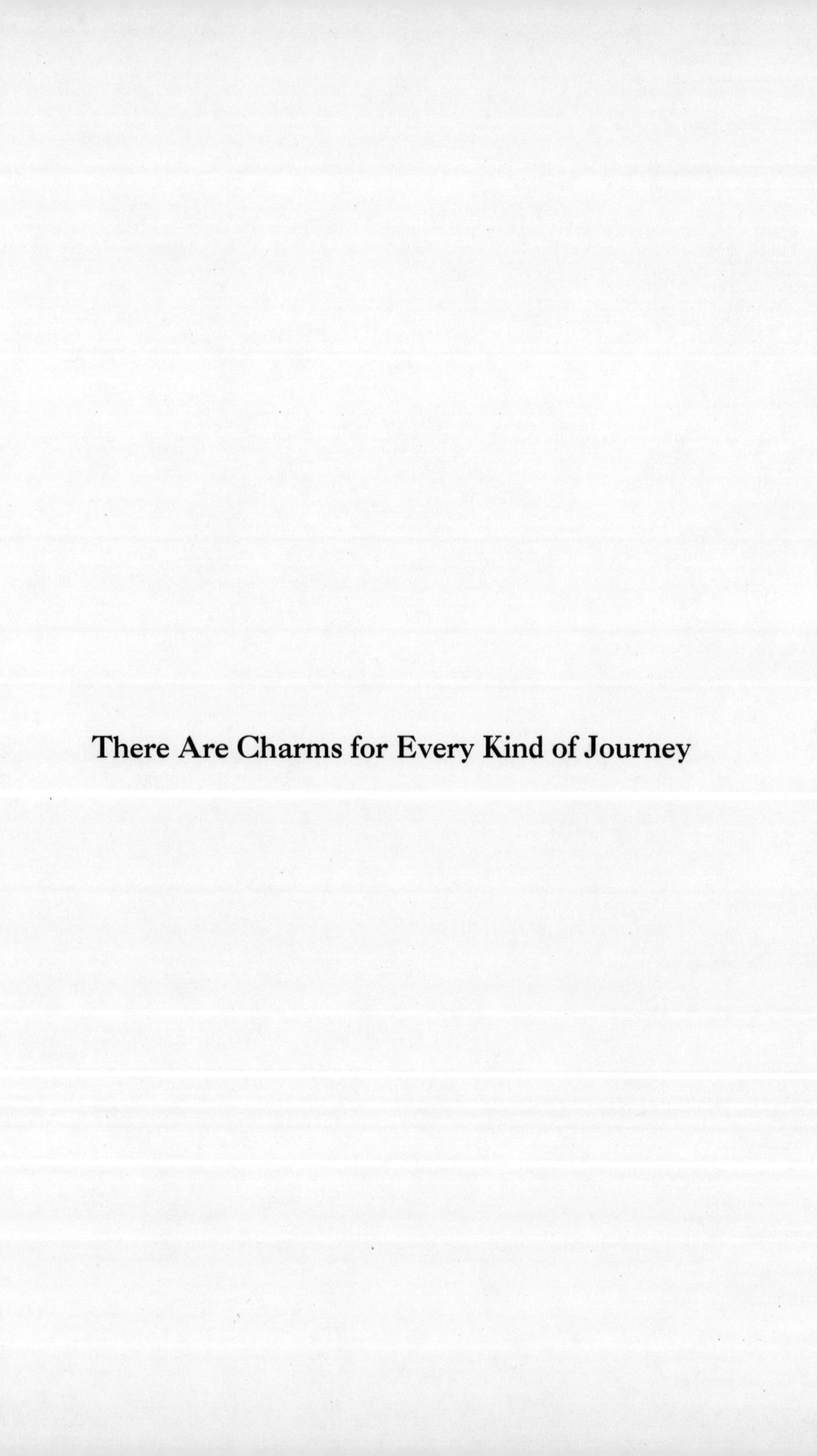

There Are Charms for Every Kind of Journey

Anne Michaels

Skin Divers

Under the big-top
of stars, cows drift
from enclosures, bellies brushing
the high grass, ready for their heavy
festivities. Lowland gleams like mica
in the rain. Wet starlight
soaks our shoes; the seaweed
field begs, the same
burlap field that in winter cracks with frost,
is splashed by the black brush
of crows. Frozen sparklers of queen anne's lace.

Because the moon feels loved, she lets our eyes
follow her across the field, stepping
from her clothes, strewn silk
glinting in furrows. Feeling loved, the moon loves
to be looked at, swimming
all night across the river.

She calls through screens,
she fingers a white slip in the night hallway,
reaches across the table for a glass.
She holds the dream fort.
Like the moon, I want
to touch places we didn't know,
just by looking. To tell
new things at 3 in the morning, when we're
awake with rain or any sadness, or slendering through
reeds of sleep, surfacing to skin. In this room
where so much has happened, where love
is the clink of buttons as your shirt slides
to the floor, the rolling sound of loose change;
a book half-open, clothes
half-open. Again we feel
how transparent the envelope
of the body; pushed through the door
of the world. To read what's inside

we hold each other
up to the light. We hold
the ones we love or long
to be free of, carry them
into every night field, sit with them
while cows slow as ships
barely move in the distance.
Rain dripping from the awning of stars.

Waterworn, the body remembers
like a floodplain, sentiment-laden,
reclaims itself with every tide.
Memory terraces, soft as green deltas.
Or reefs and cordilleras -
gathering the world to bone.

Of all the marshy places,
only the past is named.

The moon touches everything
into meaning, under her blind fingers,
then returns us to cerulean
aluminum dawns. Night,
a road pointing east.
Her sister, memory, browses the closet
for clothes carrying someone's shape.
She wipes her hands on an apron
stained with childhood, familiar smells
in her hair; rattles pots and pans
in the circadian kitchen.
While in the bedroom of a night field,
the moon undresses; her abandoned peignoir
floats forever down.

Memory drags possessions out on the lawn,
moves slowly through wet grass, weighed down
by moments caught in her night net, in the glistening
ether of her skirt. The air alive:
memory lifts her head and I nearly
disappear. You lift your head, a look I feel
everywhere, a tongue of a glance,

and love's this dark field, our shadow web
of voices, the carbon-paper purple
rainy dark. Memory's heavy with the jewellery
of rain, her skirt heavy with buds of mercury
congealing to ice on embroidered branches -
as she walks we hear the clacking surf
of those beautiful bones. Already love
so far beyond the body, reached only
by way of the body. Time is the alembic
that turns what we know
into mystery. Into air,
into the purple stain of sweetness.
Laburnum, wild iris, birch forest so thick
it glows at night, smells that reach us
everywhere; the alchemy that keeps us
happy on the ground, even if our arms embrace
nothing, nothing; the withdrawing
trochee of birds. We'll never achieve escape
velocity, might as well sink into wet
firmament, learn to stay under,
breathing through our skin.
In silver lamella, in rivers
the colour of rain. Under water, under sky;
with transparent ancient wings.

Tonight the moon traipses in bare feet,
silk stockings left behind
like pieces of river.
Our legs and arms, summer-steeped
to dark tea, slapped damp
with mud and weeds.

We roll over the edge into the deep field,
rise from under rain,
from out shapes in wet grass.
Night swimmers; skin divers.

Elizabeth Philips

Leaving the Air

Barely breaking the surface of sleep, she turns
to divine the water in me, a freshet seeping from mouth
to mouth.

But I can see the dry cold light leaking in under the door
and hear the wind scything along the eaves while three months
of snow lies heavily on the ground. Sliding onto me

she urges me to swim with her, laughing and kissing me
like a fish. I smile and run my fingers along her spine.
Outside, a plane passes over the house.

She begins then, her mouth creeping down my belly,
tangled hair draped over her eyes. I place my hands
lightly on her head.

The blood in my veins flickers like fins
in a shallow stream, and I am recalled to the beauty
of the dappled breadth of the lake, the waves

pulling me deeper. Sinking into the bed
I lose the sun and the glittering snow, and soon
see only with my skin

red blanket, damp white sheet, the rest of the room
lost in fog. Drenched in the goodness of salt, my body
is blurred, littoral,

a line drawn between the water and the land.
And then my hips rise on a wave, and I'm breathing
under-sea, a pulsing eel lying on the bottom

bearing the weight of the living water.

Barry Dempster

**Green as the Vein in a Young Man's Desire...
Eastwood 1906**

              Green as a leaf's vein.   Green as
a thumbprint in moss.   Green
as confetti on stillborn ponds
as infant grass.
Asleep in a meadow
my bare chest stains green.
The nestled loin stone
the polished jade.

Somehow the forest overwhelms
most of life.   Chestnut roots
crack kitchen floors, holly leaves
scratch downstairs doors, rabbits
eat entire dresser drawers.
I dive from my gaping bedroom window
and am instantly stripped and shrunk.

The mines grow arthritic, blacken
back to dirt and undergrowth.   The town
squats on its squalid hill and strains.
In the moonlight a young man
runs tiny in the valley; a darting
nakedness, escape.   In a bed
of violets, an exhausted embrace.

Women here turn red as berries
their slippers sinking in the leaves.
Shopgirl smiles whisked aside, strands
of scented hair.   Bare ankles
marvellous in blue brooks.   I would like
nothing better than to bleed
those berries between my fingertips.

Such are the tripping fantasies
of an Eastwood lad with the woods
set free in his nerves and wrists.
If only the world were totally green.
Men walking entire countries
with nothing hidden, blossoms
bursting in their eyes, each glance
a colour, a bouquet of flesh.

Green as the vein in a young man's
desire.   May all the lovers in the world
be smudged with fingerprints.
The forest thrives through my
bedroom window and carries me away.
Even my nipples are hard as jade.
The world sharpened to a blade of grass.

Peter Stevens

Running into Darkness

After the game, after the hide-
and-go-seek, no longer, the bored group,
the lounging, rough tumbling on the grass
in the park, the quick touches, retreats,
the girls pushing and pulling, the awkward arm
thrown around shoulder, fingers nervous
on thin dresses the girls smooth down thighs
skirts flouncing out within their circling,
the sun sinking outside the gates
balancing still on the tree tops.

Possessed suddenly by flight
I begin to run in long strides stretching
the simple whiteness of my cotton dress.
I run yet see myself as white figure
in between the trees a flicker of motion
sun broken by a mesh of leaves

Running
and I know the chase draws after me
but always keeping distance—
I do not need to look behind
for he is tied precisely to my loping run
running even with the gap between,
the gap that never alters, two of us tensed

Running
the sun split now by branches
and black bars across my whiteness through the trees
his strides in step with mine we run
our places never varying and yet elastic
light and looped together

Running
down the setting sun beyond the fence
glimmering light and heavy strides behind
my legs are slowing and he is

Running
catching closer and the slowing sun spreads gold
beneath the purple evening slowing I am never

Running
from him only with him never looking back
he seeing whiteness through the gathering
darkness black bars of trees the iron fence
is melting in his eyes

Running
with me closer now.

Running
ends, his hands are reaching out
and underneath his hands my shoulders
round and my bare arms are warm
to his warm hands—the gold is thinning
shadows merging with the darkness falling

Falling we lie together silent
breathing as two runners after racing—
no one wins or loses—space between
we sense it still within the darkness.
He turns and slowly draws his fingers
down my face across my beating heart
small roundness of my breast, dip at waist

Turning
now he moves away and off into the dark

Lying on the cooling grass I look into the night
for the first time see the moon's hard outline
the definition of the stars, distance tangible
between them

Walking
now from the park and through the dark's new light
the fence behind makes a row of swords, hilts joined,
points thrust deep into the ground.

Bill Gaston

I Send My Birds Out

Looking for you, I send my birds out
to take eaves in beak and lift the roof
of that house in your rumoured neighbourhood.
It is my right: there were promises.
Searching, I send a flock of special chickens to slaughter.
They know who eats them, and where, and even why.
Can you blame me? you took my past
and without my past I cannot land.
Closing in, the hummingbird at your window
is a camera, the beat of its wings my heart.
I am not being pathetic.
As you will see:
You on the duck pond bench alone.
The swan that glides to foot so knowingly
will show, with ancient looping of neck,
the invitation
of half a human heart.

Karen Connelly

There Are Charms for Every Kind of Journey

A bird I've never seen threads a desolate song
through this labyrinth of pines.
Dusk comes, then the indigo oil of night.
The stars are white sapphires shattered
and sinking in the black-ocean sky.
Mountains dive and rise like dolphins.
Tonight I will dream of the Bay of Biscay,
the shores where I will breathe without you.
You cannot sleep by the sea.

If you were still here, I would whisper,
          Lay your hand on my back.
I would say, I wish you wanted me more than these moments.

Train whistles pierce every black hour,
wise arrows in this witless heart.
The engines cry, Come away come away.

You once said, It's hard to lie in the mountains.
Then you lied beautifully, without blinking.

You left months ago,
I leave tomorrow at dawn.
Simplicity is the birthright of deer
who do not name days or plan betrayals.
My life is a broken bridle
and yours is an antique clock.

I wish I could have given you a talisman
whose loss wouldn't have maimed me.
There are charms for every kind of journey.
You needed an owl's black claw,
or a scorpion imprisoned in amber
or my anklebone.
But there was no time.

The trains in this deaf country
don't hold people anymore
but I'm going to find one
to drag my heart away from this valley
where you seeded love in me.

I need a train.
I need that kind of weight and roar
to rip your gentle lyrics out of my mouth.

Richard Lemm

The Arsonist

Everyone loves fires. The pleasure
in their faces is my own.
They wait in their flickering rooms
for the sirens. Better than the lottery,
the chance I will see their cast-off
clothes, ripped into rags and soaked
in that smell of our century.

I am alone in the first amber
moment, one small flame
grows like the tree
of life, red branches leaping up
out of ourselves into the night sky,
and the black smoke we have
held inside too long. Who but the owner
mourns the sacrifice of a large
wooden box and its memories
unknown to us, most likely banal.
Listen to the roof and walls
crackle, years of tedium
billow, blow.

How fast they come, those who say
tragedy, what kind of sick...
if this happened to me, and their eyes
engorge with the hot tongues
licking faster. I freed the one
spark from every ice-cold face
and bonded them together into this:
a packed circle glowing around
ashes. Me. The only one not
quite smiling.

Pier Giorgio di Cicco

On the Question of Lisa's Thighs

There is the question of Lisa's thighs
and the "consistency" of them. There is no word
for "consistency" among lovers. Jello and liquid cement
have consistency, but fingers sinking into flesh, the yield
and give is without nomenclature. So that we say
we feel good to one another. You feel "real good".
Stupid language in the hands of angels.

Dawn then, and the question of Lisa's thighs.
A metaphor would be good, like light receding
to horizon, her yield. She has walked off with her
yield and leaves the impression of it in my mind like
a plum. Bambola, I call her, because dolls are round and
dumpling like and dough has a consistency I get off
on but she's not dough. She's cloud with a flesh lining
and an icon of emotion inside.

Then there is the question of Lisa's skin; it is not milk
or alabaster, so it is like drinking spring water and
always thirsty for it.
Thank you for the spring water
which is like a mist perused by light.

Lust, untrammelled, like bravery in the lilac garden.
And voices singing in the room, which are like the muscles in
Lisa's thighs rippling into one another. Under-sea movements.
Or the taut grace of an opened fist.
My feeling is a tablet on which the first days are written.

Beauty, unworded, like a deja vue, and a romp in the garden.
A woman on top of it all, and a language that
won't suit her. Incarnations is what my mind is like
in her. And fluorescence like the way my fingers
flame when our bones lock. There will always be the
question of Lisa's thighs one morning; an epistemology
under the skin of language. Only her lips spell it, and
even they do it silently.

Gregory Scofield

He Is

earthworm, caterpillar
parting my lips, he is

slug slipping between my teeth
and down, beating

moth wings, a flutter
inside my mouth,

he is snail kissing dew
from the shell of my ears,

spider crawling breath tracks
down my neck and weaving

watersnake, he is
swamp frog croaking my chest

hopping from nipple to nipple,
he is mouse

on my belly running circles
and circles, he is

grouse building his nest
from marsh grass and scent,

weasel digging eggs
between my legs,

he is hungry, so hungry
turtle, he is

slow, so slow
nuzzling and nipping

I crack
beneath the weight of him,

he is mountain lion
chewing bones, tasting marrow

rain water
trickling down my spine

he is spring bear
ample and lean

his berry tongue quick,
sweet from the feasting

Barry Dempster

Unconditional Love

Undeniable love.   Shaking me
by the cuff in a drooling embrace,
wrapping my resistance
in an endless tail.   Squirms me
to the rug, a flash of fur,
boy becoming beast, sprouting whiskers
from behind my ear, cold noses
in my cupped palms.   Picture
homo sentimentalien and mutt.
Her tongue making territory of my body.

Almost heredity, this doggy love.
Dad and his Airedale
crossing childhood at a trot.
A great-uncle and his even Greater Dane
sharing slippers for 20 twilight years.
Cousin Helen with a Pomeranian
grinning from her black patent purse.

Who else but a dog showed me
how to hug, letting my arms go
messy, my kneecaps and navel and chin
all joining in an electric shock?
Who else could make a compliment
out of a bare belly?   Canine kisses
taught me true affection, a
stray unselfconsciousness.

Are there dogs in heaven?   I asked
my mother, an elastic band
squeezing my heart into
an upstairs/downstairs shape.

No souls is what she said.   A dog
is nothing but an instant, here and
gone.   I imagined God
all spine and loneliness, naked
as a bar of soap.

When I go, my dog will go with me.
We'll race past those staunch
pearly gates, to the Happy Hunting
Ground, the Other Side, the Abyss, whatever
it's really called.   I'd rather grow
a tail than a pair of stiff wings.
An eternity of unconditional love, that
cold-nosed, no-soul beast.

Ludwig Zeller

Woman Under the Lindens

Are you pure accord, both instrument and woman,
A flower burning in the invisible? Blindly
We look at you, and tattoo you whom we cannot see,
Creating signs to reveal you, a mirage to be your skin.
You come to us trembling as if a mystery had touched you.

I drowned myself in you and at the bottom of your eyes
Half saw the dream that we can never decipher:
Across your face floats a swarm of petals,
Music of the desire of being, to be with you,
To be the sun in the blood.

There, in a perfectly held trilling, I burned
On the pulsing snow that is your skin. The boundaries
Between words erased themselves and a graceful air touched you
From within. Tears were warm, moons were gliding down
To nest on your shoulders.

                                  Are you still there?
The days keep passing, I hear nothing but echoes,
Crumbs of ruined forgiveness, and the coming cold.

The scar of desiring you starts to hurt again.

Translated by A.F. Moritz and Theresa Moritz

Blaine Marchand

Travelling Alone

Take it, you insisted.
Your Michelin guide to ancient Rome.
Flipping open the pages carefully,
the spine broken from being well-thumbed,
you said the best ruins are the ones
you marked. Your hand lingered on mine
as I took the book, tucked it
carefully in my luggage,
smiling, imagining one day we might travel
as lovers.

Once off the plane, the taxi hurtled me
through the quiet roadways,
early morning shadows dark as priests in cassocks.
I checked into the hotel, unpacked the guide, set out.
It took my breath away,
the Coliseum, there, at the end of the street,
a broken honeycomb through which the sun poured.
You, an artist, were right.
The light here beautiful, exquisite as saffron.
From some cavern inside, pilgrims sang the Te Deum,
their voices careened among the stones,
exposed as if the venerated corpse of a martyr.

Then on to St. Peter-in-Chains. This you gave three stars.
It was dark and damp. Scaffolding everywhere
as if it were about to collapse on itself.
But off to the right, the unfinished tomb of Pope Julius,
Michelangelo's Moses. A tourist clunked a coin into the meter.
The light against the sculpted, muscled arms a shimmer of water.
I thought of you stepping out of the shower
after we had made love. You bent to the bed,
a pool of drops gathered on my chest.
For the first time, I felt the isolation
of the tourist travelling alone. Fatigue made me skittish.
I turned back to the hotel where, although only noon,
I fell into the dead of sleep.

All week long, each day, after work,
your choices guided me into basilicas,
down the Spanish Steps, through the Terme di Caracalla,
but also to less-travelled sites.
Feeling out-of-place,
among the elegant Italian men you raved about.
I thought about you and me, so similar,
craving beauty everywhere. Soothing the pain.
All our life walking among the remnants
of our past, rendering, transforming them,
the way floodlights at night
accented the monuments,
gave them surrealistic splendour.

By mid-week, I imagined us in bed once again,
waking from the brief drowse men fall into
after sex, comparing insights, impressions.
But although the plane brought me closer,
you withdrew, kept retreating,
always a last minute change of plans.
I sought guidance, explanations,
confused by your tactics, your cryptic signs.

Now I willingly wander
among the monuments of my own city.
I stare up at the flank of bronze soldiers
in the arch of the War Memorial.
The sculptor has them advancing,
a battalion of heroic men
marching through the eye of a needle.
I, too, have finally chosen to pass through.
High above, on the arc of granite,
winged Peace and Freedom hold up
a torch and laurel to the open sky.

Jan Conn

Into the Gathering Dark

A woman and a man drive a rented car
hundreds of kilometres through northern Guatemala
into the gathering dark, foolishly, intently,
the woman driving too quickly, the man

unable to speak of the few things he has come
to value. He watches a white stallion
tethered by the dusty roadside, its matted hair
suddenly coral-coloured as the sun
plunges behind a line of dark blue mountains.

Between him and the stallion, nothing.

A hologram of flies.

On both sides of the road the fields
look blasted: white soil, dry flutter of maize.

They have taken this turn-off
because several drunken men
crowded around a tiny wooden building
pointed this way. This way to Colomba

and the highway where ten years ago a truck
drove off the road, killing the passenger instantly.
The passenger who was the brother
of this man in the car.

This explains their urgency but not
the violence, rushing to meet them
in the form of stones hurled at the car windows
by the inhabitants of a small *pueblo*
because they are strangers
who could easily bring more deaths with them,
or because the stabbing white headlights
of the white rental car
are too reminiscent of the lights used
to extract information
by men who probe, electrically,
the soft inner reaches
of women by day
and the genitals of other men
by night.

Elisabeth Harvor

Bloom, Rain

How do we do it?
Learn how to be old?
When it's not what we planned on?
Once I walked down the street
with only one thought in my head (your name),
it was raining, there were tipped shelves
of boxes, they smelled of wet wood
and bananas, and the bananas were wet
and the green grapes were wet,
I was having my period (I was
always having my period
when it was raining)
and everywhere
there were umbrellas
raised up,

ruby shelters
lit by rainy-sky light,
and the mounds of the garden too,

petal-littered,
everything driven,
rained down onto the
shrapnel, the sharp stones
of the pocked lawns and gravel

and under the small
hoisted world of every umbrella,
people hurrying or plotting
(people plot more when it's raining,
a little-known fact from the annals
of rain-lore—they plan for sunlight,
they plan to be happy) and this

petal carnage, this windy
damp, these umbrellas
all had something to do
with seepage, with pelvic pain—
with pelvic pain in the rain

and me walking along
and thinking your name
while taking such comfort
in that persistent dull pain.

But now, years later, people
walk in the rain as if they
are vowing things; to listen
to more of the kind of music
that stirs the soul, for instance,
the kind of music that makes you
remember you haven't lived the
life you wanted to live—

no, I don't imagine them vowing this,
I'm too unhappy to imagine other
people vowing things, I won't
give them the credit, I'm locked
in the egomania of regretting my life,

but oh, think of it! Never again
to feel that dragged young ache
in the womb, never again to
feel that easing warm bloom
of the flood from your body

bathing me in every part
of my body—the way it tore
a cry from me, and long before this, even—
we are dancing, your hand, fingers splayed
on the small of my back and formally
steering me, heat blooming in your palm,

heat breathing
in and out of the heart
of your stilled hand,

beyond us a line
of hung shirts and sweaters
wet with the colours of fog, of goldenrod,

turning as we turn,
the day's foggy too—it's almost dark,

now it is dark...is it
raining?

Memory wants rain

the night wind
in the shot garden—

a rattling,
an unfurling,

the black windows,
rain

David Manicom

Beehive Huts

Dingle Peninsula, West of Ireland

You find them, the stone cones of the hermits,
a rough pottery of the rock-sown earth,
castings of the endless serpent Patrick drove
from the soil into the mind's nest of crosses.
His path from Rome swallowed itself behind him.

The road, slow with bikes and Peugeots, runs west
between the chanting surf and the scoured hills,
mists erases the verge of sea and sky.
You find them, suddenly, twelves centuries queer,
cold and whispering, making slow peace with the land,

curving day like Kerry's black mountains.
The gnat-bitten bodies of madmen
do not lie inside, you will not stumble on saints
who can steal the world away from your hands.
The floor is smooth with your own barrenness.

These stones, perfect for fences, are not taken,
storms have not removed one from another.
Muscles cramped, here, on the dust where your foot
is. You fear to think yet thirst to believe
that myth is this small dome, where men sat

and stared at crucifixion year after year
until seagulls became pieces of wind
and eyes, sea, sky blurred into one blue mist.
You are relieved that their yellow bones,
cracked on the edges of season, are never found.

Don Domanski

Poem for Piano and Violin

it's evening once again
and the palms of silence sway in the closet

the musician hums like a sewing machine
like God playing the music of hares
against the background of lightning and rain

it's a sad religious day
and the shoulders of his genitals
turn downward like the wings of a gull
gliding out to sea

it's Monday once again
and the house smells like an orchestra
burning away in the stove buried in the damp garden

it's a sad day
and the music turns upward
like a smile might turn if a smile were there
like a ring-finger might turn if it were sleeping
on a hand tired of grief.

Daniel David Moses

Shorts Lines

Again overnight so late in the year all bushes are bare,
just off the path, just under the underbrush, bright against sere,
bright as a flower to the first jogger—he shakes his head. Yes,

yet another pair of undershorts here. How hardy they are,
the flowers, he thinks, who keep coming out though temperatures sink.
How delicate too, this breed that goes from blooming to seed all

in a few minutes of night. And the fall from limbs through the frost
and dark at the end must be beautiful! he laughs with what breath
he can spare. He keeps running onward, sure it's familiar,

the light that forces all the opening of buds. He's seen it
before, most often in dreams, flooding the clothes the stranger there
wears like shadows. Oh he knows how moonshine can soften a fist!

And what's leftover after? His laughter in the morning sun,
his throat and his tongue, a lonely flower—except perhaps for
the one he just passed, that old blossom, torn, unforlorn cotton.

Daniel David Moses

Bus Lines

The doors of the bus sigh and open
—and who among us wouldn't? Who would
refuse the young man who boards? Could you

deny this khaki parka? Of course
he's broken our cross town trance. But watch
how he walks down the aisle and you'll

easily enter another. Hear
how the engine purrs? And the gears shift.
Oh we've travelled miles already,

out ahead of the wind. Temperatures
rise and the days unfold and those dark
eyes chance out of his hood like the first

buds from branches. How we long for long
limbs under green rain. Then a growl from
the driver, the name of a street, brings

the dream to a stop—he's up and gone.
But how glad we are, riding on, just
knowing he lives on Lavender Road.

Snow Music

Erin Mouré

The Health of Poetry
The poll tax riots, London, winter 1990

Affiched in headache tremour, such splendor, the
coat she finally wore.
The ability to pay.

The photo on the front page: a kitchen chair hurled
above the pushing crowd, caught there by the memory of
silver, which remembers

light, even for a moment
Remembers *the coat*

Who knows what is happening to the country!

2

Or do we begin, begin again, being
what we are, tremulous beings

with sucker hearts.

Eyesores. *Fideles*

3

Soft as the inseams & edges,
trammelled.

Our coats, the coats we wore.

Herringbone islands. Whispers of faint
grief, graven.

The country!

4

Graven spirit. Or,
serious. (P)tome-
aine poison.

The coat.

Flecked with rain,
this time.

5

One tax for each citizen, regardless.
The rich pay, the iron voice said
equally

with the poor, the rich having
less need of state

services.

We are, a government of
egalité, the mouth said.
Having
few colonies,
our own people become suspect.
Weakened, it said. *Treatable*

6

The health of a republic, said the metal voice
relies on those with no need of it

Whose pink glow must be protected
from the needy, whose needs corrupt
order or metal, making the state
necessary.

The kitchen chair, airbound.
Tilted slightly.

Whoever sits
tips
its balance

Beneath it, *the clamour.*

7

Hoi polloi.
Invisible cuts sewn & heads turned upward,
the people, *fideles*, necks bare
The chair hanging

Even for a moment, the rain.

To begin again, the coat such splendour,
she finally wore. Chosen. Cry out:

Ibrahim! A herringbone crease.
A herringbone.

8

Red herring.
Where's there's smoke there's fire.
The sky a kitchen for the chair.
Pull up & peel these, the metal says.
The health of poetry, it says.
Peel these skins.

Barbara Carey

Spectacles

He had stood
at the top of the world
on 7 different continents
& breathed its cirrus
thinness so often
his voice dropped
this close to sea level,
to the density
of inhabited space

he showed his slides
of peaks & terrifying
islands of height
as others display
snaps of family—
that touch of offhand
pride. & sharing
closely in a spectacle
when others can only look
upon its surface

but it went deep
with him—he had lost
other climbers, some
in the letting go
of avalanches
unpredictable as emotion,
most in the simple
loss of their own
precarious holds

& on his last ascent
of the most forbidding
approach to Everest,
had prayed
with his silent Sherpa guides

by the frozen body
of another climber,
a woman found
curled against the mountain's
flank as if taking
refuge from the bladed wind
after questions
about equipment, lenses, technique
& just when everyone
in the packed auditorium
was beginning to think
of where they had parked
the car

a woman stood & asked
why there was no photo
of the frozen climber

I think some of us
might have smothered
nervous laughter,
all of us turned
to look, as eager
to observe the questioner
as she was to see
what a practised hand
could make known
of death

later it was what
we would most
remember, & not
the 7 summits:
when that night
watching news clips
of the world's
impersonal horrors
we were suddenly
ashamed

Neile Graham

The Tree in the World

Here it is, the easy American metaphor.
The sharp, simple, (twisted) equivalency,
the words meaning death. Let me explain:
outside my window is a tree,
yes, leaves that catch and bend light,
their shadowed, secret unders, the mystery
of their autumnal transformations.
Last November after it turned,
before the brunt of winter hit it,
the landlord came with a saw and
lopped it, hacking unevenly,
not pruning but attack. Barely
more now than unsymmetrical branches
eccentrically offering their leaves
to the light, but the following spring
it sacrificed blossoms to the season.
This tree is a part of my human family.
Think of it as the poor,
attacked by the landlords, who say nuke
the Iraqis, I only rented to her because she
was from a rich family, they can't pay
the new rent, let them find another place,
that man. The misshapen branches,
the blossoms, the new leaves,
its awkward inelegance, its lumpish dance
in the wind. But this morning a cherry,
just in my reach. I picked it, dear listener,
and my lord it was sweet. It tasted alive.

Sue Wheeler

Their Futures Drift Like Ash Across the City

Triangle Shirtwaist Factory, 1911

Young women sturdy as pine trees
veins resinous with dreams
abandon needles mid-seam
in Egyptian cotton, leave
black bread radish and onion
in the chipped lunch pails, hearts
treadling terror hot as the knobs
and hinges on the locked fire escape
doors. The girl with the purple ribbon
smashes a stool through the cobwebbed
glass and they leap and leap, the sky
is a shudder of petticoats, skirts
are bells pleating the morning
air, their hair untwists and spills
above them, epiphanies of flame.
They are bridal bouquets tossed
and tossed from balconies, a Calvary
of reacing arms, fingers spread
like the ribs of the tightrope
walker's umbrella.

Claire Harris

By Thy Senses Sent Forth

By Thy senses sent forth
go right to the rim of Thy longing
give me garment.

Gregor Sebra

Awakened
       by a touch
       or a rush of wind
spreadeagled
in the red light
flaring
through the corn
lifting her head
she found herself
skewered
on the One Eye
of God
a quiet
     so intense
it was the absence
     of sound
eventually
the color faded
darkness
seeped from
the western sky
And she ran
       swiftly
cautiously
through the corn
home to hide
a spatter of rain
dodging
her footsteps

Through the kitchen window
she saw that the tropical sun
had begun to fade
the children's hour was over
"think" she said
transfigured on the braided rug
in that hot wooden room
the Bible closed in her hand
"think of the cool benediction of snow"
and seeing bright inquiry on their faces
"a down   a sort of icy down
billions of feathers"
and felt a fleeting pity

He worked alone   his green face tho' knotting into righteousness
still smiled easily   he refused to acknowledge the heat the rains
the wild tropical growing   even as he laughed about her open fear
of giving birth alone (the baby and her entrails in a stream of
blood   he taking her intestines in his curling fingers to put them
back)   It had not happened except in his dreams   and she still
feared   He grew luxuriant   had won or almost won   his
gardens bloomed flooded the sparse markets   still each night he
searched the Bible and his conscience joked at her wittled his
gifts and waited for   Saturday while the years folded over him
like the scales on an armadillo   Fixed he supposed her always
to be found   he grew careless of love   commanding her to a
son she gave him seven daughters

In that land her fair skin burnt to a quick maturity she learned
early how to use suffering to weave the heart's invisible tales
to make out of that green boredom a home   content in her
own unease she sometimes prayed   While he worked the wide
fields cndlessly

Years later
that sunset
dimmed by age
its metaphor drawn
by experience
gradually
she found herself
in a desolate place
without horizon
or color
hers was the sustained
noiseless terror
of an abandoned child
under the burden of furnishing
the empty rituals
she grew frivolous
longed to savor every edged
delight   One day
the dust began to settle
possessed of craftsman's hands
she furnished a Builder
she adopted the Shadows
of Myth   the poetry of others
till possessed of metaphor
she found
The word was made flesh

In His Name
before night swooped down
over the pioneer farms
she would pick
the purple berries for jam
and hasten home
before the unborn/undead
left their cave of leaves
to call piteously in the twilight
before the plumed serpent
soft as a dove from the trees
lest she answer
inspite of crosses
so become the fable
told in the yellow light
of kerosene lamps

All that afternoon the baskets on
her arm she moves through the sprung
gate   moves over and over   to walk
outside the secure   fences   often she
drifts there her feet not touching the
ground the gate swinging open at
her glance clicks shut
she is
beyond the
perimeters of
the farm and all its
tame gardens where the bell
peppers hang   free from wrath   in
Saskatchewan   she drives to school between
fences   a horse drawn sleigh bundling with
straw and bricks section after section   till
the acres of open bush where the berry plants
cluster near a ditch   dense dark profusion
here everything grows so easily   even death
and sees Naomi her first born weeding in the
shimmering South American summer the beautiful
hair clinging to her neck as she dreams of end-
less acres of cool white snow   her hands swift
and sure on the purple fruit the basket
almost filled   she thinks suddenly
"she is going home" sees the
prairie grass in the
hot summer
breeze   so never hears the warning
rattle misses it again and again   drawn
towards the wild darkness of the open mouth
the infinite allure   for that lethal second she

stares then the strong body trashes
and coils in her hands   They struggle
there together in the bleak green silence
wide prairie summers her brothers hunt
rattlers with a forked stick while she
searches the hot rocks calm she turns
to outrun the swift coil the second strike
gives vent   screams a wild abandoned tram-
pling release Homeward the air dark with the
raven   his wings   his short scream as he
dives into the fields *prey*   sunflowers
pray snow billions of tiny feathers black
drifting over her
                        melting in her hair the
young Eastern teacher
                        standing her before a mirror
to frame her face
in a new style
her father
bearing the doorway like Moses
while the husband he chose weeps and
returns the babies to her swelling belly
one by one   where she lies alone giving
birth again and again in the awful heat and
viper darkness From the side open mouth
in her past streams and flickers among
the shinning leaves   her skirt

f l a r i n g   f l a r i n g   f l a r i n g

to catch the flaming frangipani the purple lunies the down
that spills from her womb   while her father watches darkly be-
hind the new window panes

Her search
tempered to the summons
of his flesh
lost its sting
the frequent children
flat like the illustrations
in fairy tales
precipitous
towards the banal
she welcomed this
sleep
But soon enough
the air stretched and tucked
itself over on earth
stabbled in some abandoned
corner of the galaxy
and she wildfire
in her own storm flared
and shifted
now-guttering
now leaping to sear all
their horizons
She needed flight
she needed new spaces
from which to search
she imagined herself walking
through some other tamed and foreign field
in the cool of the evening
and in the ancient silence
touching Him

They laid her
to rest
the ceremony
like a thin sip
of sacramental
wine
afterwards
the rains came
the dust settled
the hot vivid vines
thrust tips
like spears
through the small
grave

Bronwen Wallace

Treatment

For the doctors it seemed
simple as an old war
even the drug they used
mechlorethamine
a derivative
of mustard gas dripped
into her veins
as she lay
arms outstretched
the chemical burning into her
an older ritual
given a new name
demons to be exorcized
a witch in need of cleansing

And somehow it was
all familiar   the white tiles
and bright paint of the clinic
not unlike the kitchen
where her mother stood
and the doctor's voices
reminiscent *easy now*
there's a good girl   no tears
now big girls don't cry
or yell
not unlike her own kitchen
smells of breakfast and
her hands clenched around
her coffee cup
as the voices of her children
husband pulled at her
claws against her skin
till she snapped herself to
the good mother
the perfct wife rising

to find mittens neckties
her smile stitched across
whatever rose in her throat
and the coffee in her cup
thickened

So she told no one of her dream
witch dream where she shrank
to the size of a snail
and journeyed the warm seas
of her blood   found her womb
fragrant with moss and ferns
or how in her chest beyond
the place where her heart
shone like a blue jewel
something dark and
colder than silence
unfolded its deathscent
mingling with the smell
of ferns

didn't tell   didn't tell
how she rushed out
through her mouth and
forced it shut around
this double blossoming
while the doctors talked
of healing   her flesh
loosened and her hair
came away
in handfuls

E.D. Blodgett

vulture

who ate achilles? and what huge
scraps of war? who plucked
the bright flesh of his thighs

and ripped the idiot soft eyes
where they turned
the sun to other stars
removed?

what did the lord theseus know
and orpheus once the song
breathing scentless asphodel
where great arms of the heroes

piecemeal fell
walking in the ravenous mouth
and falling where the sun
golden never falls?

there are the ends of war
restored. there do they sit
at peace under glass

some dark with their horse
against a field of white
and some encased alone
as gazelles and poised

to fly into the wall
of pampas. here would they see
glass consuming air

all gloss gone. here
terror stopped, and knees
unclean and heaped, thus

cities, thus mere
femurs conclude, the names
spoken never
break silence here.

bird, immortal bird, you are
where the shades are cast
again, and night

come back again, your eyes
reflecting the flesh of boys
and girls singing codas to fathers

of the suns worn
crystal and transient again
where the crows blinking walk

fields of the golden fall.

Christopher Wiseman

Dead Angels

No more dancing on heads of pins
Or sunning themselves on sunlit clouds.
No more celestial music in our dreams,
Bending near the earth with harps of gold,
Standing high with trumpets over congregations.
And something else will have to be assigned
To be the guardian of children's souls
And give protection from nightmares or hunger.

For these are dead angels I look at
In a monastery storeroom, where a key
And curiosity have led me. Half-dark,
The air hot and thick, blinds drawn on the sun,
Here, among assorted relics of the years,
Among fly corpses and damaged furniture,
Are four angels in a corner, line astern,
Tilted awkwardly together in the silence.

I'm not surprised the monks didn't smash them.
I couldn't. It would be desecration,
Seeing the blue robes, the Victorian doll
Faces, the white and pink and gold,
The long feathered wings furled right down
Their backs. But see the thick dust coating
The bright blue eyes and caught in the folds
Of feathers. A shock. There's been a great fall here.

These presences should never turn to dust,
Nor be piled up, grounded, silenced, abandoned
In such a place. What monstrous innodation!
Compelled, I move around. In the shadows
The wings are deformities, turning them
Suddenly into cruel ugly three-foot birds,
All their softness gone, except in imagination's
Memory. Lilies that fester. I think of Rilke

And wait for pity to come, real compassion,
For this is wrong. These are images of light,
Of higher places, the miraculous. These
Are the singing from other worlds, the poems,
The glory shining round. Demystified, they
Stare unblinking in a clog of dust and cobweb,
Sad forsaken spirits who have filled our books
And paintings, cast gold on our history,

And can never be obsolete, for we all crave
To be spirit, to shuck off the dying animal,
To fly amazed, athiest or believer, in high music,
Transfigured and grateful. We hate
Our gross misshapen entanglements,
Our crude limitations, and look for what
Angels signify — light in darkness, music,
And brightness linking us to something else.

But I wonder if it isn't in some way
Salutary to find places like this
And contemplate how glory turns to dust,
Free flight to helpless immobility.
Perhaps we should know about dead angels,
Dead dreams, dead music, all the airless rooms
Where lambent hopes end up, and beauty, and see
How far we've fallen from the celestial,

How heavy we are, how mired, how *lumpen*.
I don't know. One last look. they smile their dusty
Doll-smiles. The shadows play tricks. A lone fly
Lurches heavily behind a blind. I must leave,
Full of dark obsequies. But then, as
I step outside, bright birds, blue and white and gold,
Unfurl their wings and swoop and soar in a great
Cloud, their songs pealing and belling

In pure enormous harmonies, not strange
To the heart, and I lift my eyes up high to them,
My spirit soft and open to the summer,
And compassion finally breaks for what
Is behind me in that room of death,
Compassion breaks as if I were released,
And it is wide as all the sky and glorious.
I stand astonished, half blinded by the sun.

Saskatchewan

Roger Nash

Circumstantial evidence of the visitation of angels

On the evidence of one hill
and several passing clouds,
there were only two of them.
Under an unprepared, but nevertheless
dark blue sky,
they met by the trees at the edge
of the field. Her cotton dress
rustled, and seemed eager
to cast shadows entirely
on its own. His forehead was uncertain.
Her eyes and freckled knees
were absolutely final. They walked
through the tall grasses of the field,
and lay down in them. After that,
we couldn't see properly.
But there was a tumult of red hair,
and nearly grey. It was as though
the whole field revolved
around them, like a water-wheel
urged on by eager oxen.
They came to have at least
six legs, and wings
from nowhere. They performed feats
like charioteers. When they left, the whole
field was doing deep breathing
and floating exercises. Afterwards,
there were no sad animals.
But the sky was completely abandoned,
along with one high-heeled
shoe in the grass, which still
fills, after rain, with cherubim
peddling clouds like bicycles.

Florence McNeil

Still Life

Lewis Carroll steeped in the wonderland
                    of early photography
determined to keep his friend Alice   his inspiration
as still as the child
sleepwalking through the pages of his book
enticed Alice Liddell
into his studio
posed her patiently by velvet tunnels of
settees
sent up
smoke and light   snapped stories
out of the air   green and exciting as Christmas crackers
uncurled the square box that would house Alice
more desperately than the four corners
of the looking glass world
the Dean's daughter   ten years old   sat seriously
her eyes black as the reeds of the
imaginary stream they rowed upon
stepped later into Carroll's darkroom where
on the book sized plate
the evidence of little Alice accumulated slowly
He took her outside   by hedges and ivy
picnicked her in the glassy boat
gazed with admiration as her hands brushed the oars
pleaded with her to remain
she looked at him as if he weren't there
and disobeying his pleas
grew bigger and bigger
and meeting her when she was thirteen
remembering the cherub
who covered his mind like the chaste filigree nudes
on a Valentine card
he was to say
she is changed a good deal
and not for the better
and the mythic black-haired girl
fading into a grey-haired print was to
remember Mr. Carroll mainly as the story-telling don
poker faced and straight
who taught her how to row.

Stephanie Bolster

Virginia Woolf's Mother in the Blurred Garden

*After the photograph, "A beautiful Vision, June 1872," by Julia
Margaret Cameron; it depicts Cameron's niece, Mrs. Herbert
Duckworth, later Mrs. Leslie Stephen, mother of Virginia Woolf.*

Ten years before your birth, you already live
in her face, in the sharpness of her nose,
the omniscience of her eyes. Your longing for solitude

permeates her, emanates from her like moonlight
to blur the camera's focus.

Behind her, blossoms quiver, shrink
into their nightly state, leave her alone.

You are not even thought of, and yet she is thinking of you
here with the tendrils of vine at the nape of her neck.
Her eyes sting with salt wind, though the sea
is miles distant, the air draped and still.
She sees, as if through layers of gauze

or water, desires worn to ragged
skin beneath waves. She widens her eyes
against crying, and the shutter opens

her into permanence. Light spills from her
like ocean water. The mouth

of time gapes wide
and chokes.

Don Coles

Our Photos of the Children

Twenty years have gone by since we took
these photos of the children, all three
together on a beach. They look up
from their beach which flows endlessly

towards you out of the front of every shot—
you can see that only a few footprints mar
the early-morning newness, and although you cannot
hear them you know that the cries of gulls are

here too, only being intercepted by
the photos' glossy surface. Based on all
the evidence, this pancake-flat lake and cyclorama of blue
sky, it's going to be a hot day. How small

they look, we say, and along with time's preposterous
gulf comes a minute of relief, thinking how much
safer they are now, being grown—
because there were always such

fears when they were little! Fears that, oh well, hard
to remember what, all of them would just stray
off-screen we suppose, or sicken inscrutably,
or be hurried into a car one day

before we'd even noticed the idling,
and then gone, we'd be without
them forever. All of which, even though
you don't ask, has in fact come about—

look, we *have* lost them!—the three slender
swimsuited figures so steadfastly
standing here ducked out of sight
long ago, and will certainly

never be back. Taking
with them when they went the last
of the little dramas they used to
keep us entertained with on our fast-

tracking through the middle of our lives,
ad *hoc* scenes such as the recurrent, every
summer at least twice, heaping of sand-dams
across the shallow stream you can see

silvering just behind them there. How
many mornings, July after July, we
laboured on these! And how seldom,
since then (and although obviously

this is an aside, it is also a lament) has
anybody anywhere been half as willing
to listen when we're in our counselling
mode, offering

our usual Grand Vizier wisdom about
whatever-it-is—in this case,
how, no matter now fast you heap u p
the sand, all in one place

or swiftly in from both side, it'll
never stop the stream on its own,
if this thing's to work you're going to
need the kind of stone

that will sit up against the flow and not just
roll away, see? therefore, the flatter
on at least one side the better, see? *O, I see. Alright.*
And although it doesn't matter

where you walk below the dam, when
you're above it try to move around without
too much splashing, OK? *OK I'll try.* No, that sort of
listening, so world-cancelling, went out

of fashion around here when the last dam went down,
and will never be back. Same with the rest of the lilliput stuff,
the little bent rakes and shovels, the unbent because
barely-used sieves, more than enough

sand-moulds and mini-pails because that's what
the weekend guests usually brought—
there was even one left-in-the-rain ark with
pairs of everything, plus a lot

of random and chipped and limbless
and generally not really useful muss—
somebody treasured these things once, but
nobody does not, unless it's us.

So what's to learn here? Only how short a time
these three small ones chose to stay
around? Only how flat the lake was when it
halted for a second there? Only how hot the day

felt, how wide and long the impersonal sand
looked? That cloudless day, and brooding under
it, vast Time—what a marshalling of hosts against
three hurrying-past ones! No wonder,

after such phalanxes, such serried
burnishings and dreadfully
nodding plumes, none of them's left!
So yes, answering the question, probably

this is all we've learned—which doesn't mean
we don't glimpse interestingly, now and then, in
our sleep, these three inflexible ones
behind their glossy torrent of clear time—

though which, if the dream will harden
and if both of us goes on trying,
one day maybe we'll drift towards these words
you're watching: day starts, a gull's first crying,

and then the dream permits that sage advice, quick
nods, a young assenting voice that still condones
whatever's said or done to stem the rising stream and show
the sand, the caution above the dam, the flatly pleasing stones.

Sharon Hawkins

A Woman is Drawing Her Mother

She sets out
five blue Staedtler pencils
sharpens each one to a point
touches them tentatively

soft ones to weave the shadows
harder ones for lines and seams
and edges
she is not an artist
is not good at this

she has erased her mother's face
ten times now
so it shines   illusory
like the face of a saint
in a holy picture

has worn the paper
thin as onion skin
in places
where the layers have lifted
around the eyes
about the mouth

she draws familiar strangers
a woman looking past her
another staring at the ground
she knits her mother's brow
she draws the back of her mother's head
she covers her mother's face
with aging hands

she draws a woman who is waiting
expectantly   for something
to happen

draws in convoluted lines
a young woman
who could have been her grandmother
and an old woman who   given time
might be herself

a woman draws her mother
slowly from memory's spool
threads her
painstakingly
through the small elusive eye
of a needle in her mind.

Carol Malyon

blurred buffalo

as though we watch them from a distance of years or memory or
tears

they fade in & out of the landscape of our minds   like memories
we almost remember   legends we heard as children & still want
to believe in

buffalo roam everywhere   on maps: buffalo new york buffalo
jump saskatchewan   in faded snapshots: tepees the fringed
jacket on buffalo bill

shaggy buffalo heads contain all the wisdom that's worth knowing

they just stand there & dream their buffalo dreams   think
philosophical buffalo thoughts   they brood on history

they munch on buffalo grass & consider mathematics   wonder: if
all the buffalo in the world gathered inside a field how large a
space would they take?

they shit big buffalo chips that no one gathers to burn as fuel

then lift their great heads & look around   bored with each other
thinking they might as well be cows   brown swiss maybe   or
jerseys   relaxing until milking or the butcher

they dream their hindu dreams of wandering village streets
sacred   forbidden to be eaten

then wake up   remember they're only out-takes from a western
movie   cluttering the cutting-room floor

or pages from a paperback by louis l'amour: mesquite
sagebrush   a tenderfoot sky-lined on a hill-top
apaches silent patient waiting a lonesome woman
fastens love-notes to tumbleweeds & lets them go

buffalo hunters wear buffalo robes   carry heavy sharps buffalo
guns   tell stories of the old days   stampedes   thousands upon
thousands   running past all day   shaking the ground like
earthquake or thunder

now the buffalo are tired   who wouldn't be?   blurred   weighed
down by history   sepia photographs   paint   melting into a
western sunset of dinosaurs   billy the kid   & all that myth

from a painting by milt jewell

Brian Bartlett

Museum Radiance

"man's hat, ca. 1740"

for A. G. Bailey

1

Impossible to touch without breaking glass,
black fur with ear flaps
rests there, dumb—a castaway
in empty space.
                    The lack of a story
becomes hard to bear. Waiting
I call forth farmers up the Nashwaak
reviving a tribal memory:

Before snowy wind flogged their coats
settlers barely raised simply shelters
in a clearing humble as a deer yard.
Lake ice grew too thick
for fishing holes, cold lips touched
hot foreheads, bits of bread soaked up
squirrel-meat grease. Diseases were storms
within storms.
                    And the dead where hung
in the trees until spring, too frozen
for ravens, too high for wolves.

2

A hat under glass is a hat under glass
but I will not stop there.
Starving does, Scottish laments,
monstrous trees, the empty space...

In spring, what a crop of burials!
Who had ever seen such pine cones?

In summer, children grappled up into
those trees, shouted across a valley
more tangled than any map,
licked sap from their hands.

One boy found his father's hat up there
and wore it for days, defied
the season. His cream-pale face
burned, the heat of play
like a January fever.

Diana Brebner

The Sparrow Drawer

1. The Sandhill Crane

The sandhill crane, in his glass case, performs
his nuptial dance. Jumping, bowing, and wildly

flapping, reads the museum description. Well,
aren't we all the same in love. This dead

male is frozen in the pose, on a bed of
stone. Thus, the museum welcomes us to its

permanent exhibit: *Birds in Canada*. When I
bring my daughters to the museum, because

it is cleaner and easier than a day in the
bush, they always ask to see the birds, or the

big animals. And I tell myself: this will
do them good. They know enough about mud,

rain, being hungry, no toilets, and wanting
to go home. In the real world, a bird is

always gone before my two-year-old can look.
Or, alternately, I can never find the great

blue herons they insist are really there.

II. Birds By Number

In the *Eastern Hardwood Forest* thirty three birds
are mounted on log pedestals, each in a pose

that is meant to be life-like. I remind myself
these are dead bodies. I have no memory for

useful things, but I can remember my first
sighting of migrating snowbirds (Junco hyemalis)

in Algonquin Park, the Rose-breasted Grosbeaks
at the feeders near the cabin, the enormous

black and white Pileated Woodpecker (Dryocopus
pileatus) with its blood-red crest, up near the

cliffs at Luskville. I can tell you where, and
who was with me, down a great-list of the birds

I believed forgotten. My daughters learn birds
by numbers, matching a numbered body with a

name on a list, given in three languages, as if
that will make them real. The fact is, my girls

enjoy this. They call them doll-birds. And the
bird names are repeated solemnly, as if each

name were part of a spell. And I do it too.
For who can say this is not reverence, a litany,

a prayer, a wish for something promised. The
name of one woman who died finds its way to

the list, and I remember my first sighting of a
                rare old man I loved.

III. The Sparrow Drawer

It is time for us to be leaving. Somehow we find
ourselves before one final display. It is the same

forest, rearranged by seasons, and including
the ducks, herons, owls, and hawks, that are

familiar to *The Forest*, as they call the example of
hardwood forest that is local, and ours. And then,

beneath the glass cases, my eldest daughter finds
two drawers. Above them a simple label reads:

Would you like to know more about birds? How
many times did I bring that other child to this

place? We never found these boxes. And they
are not hidden, merely unexpected. The first

lights up as we pull it out. Eggs. Large and
small. Blue, green, mottled beige, brown. Great

white goose eggs, the hummingbird's egg glowing,
a white pearl, all in rows, labeled, an old child's
                    collection.

And the second drawer opens quietly, and as easily
as the first, lights up, displays its contents.

This is the sparrow drawer. No-one has gone to any
trouble to make this look pretty. Dead sparrows

lie in an uneven row, their bodies in disarray,
frozen on snow, which is also synthetic batting,

with black plastic arrowheads stuck in strategic
areas to accentuate their differences. The caption

tells us: all sparrows look alike to the untrained
eye. They are difficult to tell apart in the field.

Chipping Sparrow. Savannah Sparrow. Lincoln's Sparrow.
Song Sparrow. Swamp Sparrow. And alone, beneath

the line of identical bodies, a Pine Siskin, just
to show us how even one species can be mistaken for

another. And what have I seen hovering in a field?
I could swear it was the child I have lost. Love

I have learned the hard way; how many hovering boys
in schoolyards look just like him. Of course, I don't

want to see this, or the dead birds, and I close
the drawer. But my girls will not leave it alone.

They open it. I close it. They cry. So, we open it
again. We say the names of the different sparrows.

I tell them that any creature, once named, cannot
be forgotten. This, I believe. You see, there are

no numbers there, only names. The Pine Siskin trembles
at the bottom of the drawer, as we roll it shut.

Lala Heine-Koehn

The Recalled Hours

Time has left, carrying bags full of waste
on his thin shoulders. Bog is bubbling up
from under the rock on which my house stands,
spilling over my garden, through the spikes of the black
iron gate, a sluggish stream following sullenly
the consumptive Pied Piper, leaving behind
the residue of what cannot be recalled.
All loveliness, smothered, is now silent.

I push aside a corner of my curtains. The stars
huddle in the darkening sky. On my doorstep,
the untrodden hours are waiting for me
to come and pick them up as if they were a new pair
of pink slippers left shyly by someone who is not sure
of the size I wear.

Robin Skelton

Snow Music

for Alison

1.

December rain
drives through the cherry tree
and flutters at our pane
insistently.

The pallid sun
is half concealed by cloud.
We turn the stereo on,
abrasive, loud.

We switch on light
in evey desperate room;
the day is almost night
in this dank gloom.

The hours are slow.
Our minds grow huddled, small.
We dream new-fallen snow
white over all.

Will it not come?
As if half-crazed by sorrow
the rain-drips drum, drum, drum.
Perhaps tomorrow

dawn will surprise
us with a stiff white plain,
new-made and still, that lies
without a stain

all round about
this weary house of night,
letting the prisoners out,
renewing light.

2. Kyrielle

The sky is dark; breath pierces, chill;
there is no wind; the trees are still;
our legs are leaden, thoughts are slow.
How will we answer to the snow?

We shared the scurrying careless Spring,
the Summer's fervent blossoming,
the Fall's excesses - all that show;
how will we answer to the snow?

Our many-coloured hurrying days
obsessed us with their vivid ways,
but now all coloured things must go;
how will we answer to the snow?

Destruction threatens from the grey
oppression of the thickening day.
Are we to lose this world we know?
How will we answer to the snow?

It asks what we have made and done
beneath the now extinuished sun.
Did we go where we meant to go?
How will we answer to the snow?

We answered Spring with lechery and
the Summer with a grasping hand,
the Fall with greed. That being so,
how will we answer to the snow?

3. Lai

Now snow is falling
and earth's a sprawling
whiteness
as drifts are hiding
sidewalks and sliding
brightness,
accept the teeming
world and its gleaming
rightness;

accept the shining
silence that, smiling,
steals us
away into seeming
contentment; dreaming
seals us
with peace, fulfilling
hope, and, stilling,
heals us.

4.

Swaddled in snow,
the laurel bush
humps a white hill
in morning's hush.

Muffled and still,
the shining street
provides no guide
for trudging feet,

distinctions lost,
for sidewalks lie
securely hidden
from the eye.

Muted and slow,
the passing cars
are all that's left
of what was ours,

the only bright
familiar shapes
within a strangeness
that escapes

all usual thought,
become a dream
in which what is
may only seem,

and every cry
we hear is thin
and meaningless
as we begin

again to learn
that all we know
is changeable
as drifting snow.

Bronwen Wallace

Sorceress

Dying made everything possible
the way the morning sun
tipped her breakfast tray
and the day rose slowly
shaped to her hands like fresh bread

below her the house moved dreamlike
through its own waking
the sounds of breakfast
voices of husband children
lapped gently against her closed door
and receded
left her to herself
neither wife nor mother
nor adult
she lived like the first inhabitant
of a new city and gathered
its magic for her own

she wore her dying
like a sorcerer's cape
and powerful with wishes
disguises she became
the mad wife in the attic
the heartless stepmother
explored again
the pure anger of childhood
cups shattered at the wall
the pieces swirling
in her screams

Daily she was child and sorceress
clothed in forbidden shapes of herself
and daily she learned
the source of her magic
saw in the mirror how
she grew more beautiful
grew vast and complex
become the city
she inhabited

And returning to the house
laid out for her like a holiday
she saw for the first time
exactly how the light lay
on the kitchen table
how the beauty of her children's faces
felt sharp as birth pains
and the days then glistened
with games
the stories her children brought
their wishes lay in her hands
like the bright dreams
of circus monkeys
and sometimes in the evenings
watching the warm shape
of her husband's hands
as he poured wine
she would spin again
in her radiant dance
and breathless see
across the water-shimmering room
the wine's ripe crystal fruit
held like a wish
at the delicate tip
of her reaching

Don McKay

Bone Poems

I

Mind is crossed, above
by clouds, below
by their fallen brothers, the bears: brown, black
cinnamon and grizzly.
Busy as tugs
they tow their moods across the screen.

But body is the home of a birch wood
whose limbs are unwritten-upon paper, listening
motionless

full of dance

II

Of all your secret selves, it is the most remote, communicating
in the intimate, carrying timbre of glaciers and French horns.
Its unheard hum arrives at inner ear without passing the recep-
tionist. Mostly we are tuned to the heart (passion, drugs,
intrigues, attacks), but it is through the bone self that the deaf
hear symphonies, that mothers know beforehand that their
children are in trouble, and that we maintain our slender diplo-
matic ties with the future and the dead. Bones attend to deep
earth, while your heart is learning, year by year, to listen to
your watch.

III

Outcrops. A lost
civilization hinted at by cheekbones.
Little is known, except
they know how to be lost. Apparently
where we have closets
they had porches.
Everything blew off.
Experience was complete combustion, hence
the scarcity of ash or
personality:

their minds unstained glass
windows, delicately veined
as wings of dragonflies

IV

Antler

Holy Cow. Some creature
so completely music that its bones

burst into song.
Now we understand these stories of the savage

pianist, annually growing hands
that stretch three octaves reaching for the loon's cry fingers

sprouting from their fingers, brilliant
failures thrown out each December.

Truly, we will also lose ourselves in forest,
wearing our lawn rakes fanned above our heads, tines

turned toward its darkness,
listening for the lost arpeggio.

V

Vertebral Lament

More orders from the star chamber: Higher! Straighter!
To us, the once proud horizontal race of snakes.

Fuck their empire. Remember the amputation.
Recite the remnants of our alphabet, Atlas to Lumbar,

meditating on the lost ones. Query, Sylphid, Zeno,
how they listened and lashed the air and

taught us poetry and danced, far
lither than the arms of maestro as

attired in his pathetic morning coat
he writhes upon the podium.

VI

Now we know the price of x-ray:
if you want to see your bones you have to
flirt with death a little. Moon-bathe.
Anticipate their liberation from your flesh.

Once upon a time
shoe stores had peepshows that could
melt your skin and show the bones
inside your feet (plenty of room for him to grow there,
ma'am). You looked down zillions, back
into an ocean where a loose
family of fish was
wriggling in blue spooky light.

There are other worlds.
Your dead dog swims in the earth.

VII

One day you will have to give yourselves
to clutter and the ravages
of air and be
no good for nothing and forget
how de ankle bone connected to de shinbone and de
word of de lawd. Truthless
you will lie in the kingdom of parts among
Loosestrife, Nightshade,
Pokeweed.
You will learn the virtues of your former enemies,
the sticks and stones, and bless
the manyness of rain.
In some other lifetime you may work
as a knife, a flute, a pair of dice, a paperweight
or charm.
Meanwhile forgive the *rasp rasp*
of the teething wire-haired
terrier.

Gonzalo Millán

Winged Fish

The fisherman raises
an underwater kite
which, stretching the line,
is lost from view
in the clouded sky.

Its resistance roots
the trees in the clouds,
turning the mountains
in the distance upside down
like a wolf's tits.

When the line breaks
the world has made one complete turn.
And the overturned dock
rests in its place,
a table with legs sticking up.

The fisherman reels in the line.
the fish, unrestrained,
tastes the painful
triumph which freedom
leaves in its mouth.

Translated by Annegret Nill

Roo Borson

The Observatory

1

The black filigree
of firs; a few stars mapping out
the fallen body of this century,
we can see almost the whole thing now,
the way a certain melody
can put the squeeze on a memory, the way
love can't be reconstructed
or channeled,
the way a bird and a tree
size up the cold, solitary,
and humans gather in rooms
in a ritual of togetherness,
or certain men are willing
to build on a mountain
to see the stars better.
We aren't made of anything you could put a name to.

2.

What happens to those
who gaze all night
at the night
who study
things beyond them
only
holding close the things that can't be had
and those
who continue all their lives
the list
of what they want
what comes of their fingertips
their eyelids
the details of their lives
where do they ever go?

The earth collapses forever
like a huge crowd waving goodbye
the stars lay their long white fingers over our eyes
making the head a cold chasm
making it the point
called nowhere.

3.

When the magenta blooms were collapsing,
when the clouds were all packing up and moving off,
did you remember the stars
behind the daylight,
what women did you touch,
how well could you love them
thinking of the galaxies, of their
tremendous speeds away from you,
and you all the while
learning adolescence, learning
a few things like how to kiss.

4.

The crossed lights of stars
like radios
turned on to different stations,
and we overhearing everything,
able to make out none of it,
our hearts
clocking our time on earth
and our departure
which is not departure
but simply the moment at which
our bodies will fall to the earth
having lost control.

The moon crawls over the ground
through a hundred hunched landscapes at once,
see how it aims for your eyes
as it does for the faces of ten thousand men,
never once missing.
It is the natural thing
to want to fill your mind
with the space between stars
and to fill your hands
with the flesh of your own kind,
the starlight
turned flesh
after thirty billion years.

5.

Below the black looming firs
we stand picking out constellations
though they aren't there
we see them with our own eyes
the way a cat will chase
a bit of nothing through the air
no one sees it but him
it's his own little game
with nothingness.

6.

When the starlight seeks you out in your own bed
what do you say to it
do you recount
the small miseries of the day
what good does it do
to lie there not sleeping
just watching the hills change shape
as the earth
rolls slowly under the starlight sheets
the cycles
of being a creature

getting up for the sunlight
and lying down
as you've been taught
not knowing any better
or any other
what good it is to be
merely the way things happen
an explosion
and finally the tiny earth with you on it.

7.

There is a light strangling in the treetops
shadows
like trapdoors
in the rough grass
or the doorways to root cellars

they are for appearance's sake only
they remind us
there are doors we will not enter

somewhere in the long line
of descendants we see in each other's eyes
between the universe that invented us
and its end
a light that strangles
in the treetops
the slash of wind
cattle ants seedpods
all the live jewelery moving upon the earth

having lain for an hour and tried to dream
the universe before and after all this
what is there to do now
but stumble back into the deep sleep
of love-making of eating
of being creatures again.

8.

A few birds flicker
through the silt of dusk
to their homes
wherever they build them
in the matrices of branches

the hills holding
silence like a lens

the few bird cries
magnified

the hills grow heavy
after the ardour of grasses
clawing their one inch toward outer space
as the shadows leak into the cleavages

the moon
which is a stone
climbs into the eye
of the observatory

9.

July
a black sky
knifed by lightning
and the bleating of thunder
the city hazy
with rain-coloured lamps leading down to hell,
the round horizon
crazed
like a broken bowl
of swords,
swords breaking over the hunched backs of peasants.

The observatory in the storm
is a shut white eye
No one moves inside it,
it is empty of everything except instruments,
and they lean back on their stands
empty of thought,
preferring this lull to the endless
survey of stars,
going out a little farther each year.
They would almost rather
humans not want to know
anything more,
so they could just do nothing for a long while.

Even on a night like this,
everything gone wild
just because of a little wind,
a little thunder,
the observatory stays sane,

the only thing to gauge
the true depth of the night.

Contents Publishing History

The following indicates in which issue of *Arc* each contribution to *We All Begin in a Little Magazine* originally appeared.

Arc 1, Autumn 1978
"vulture," E. D. Blodgett

Arc 3, Autumn 1979
"Still Life," Florence McNeil
"Running into Darkness," Peter Stevens

Arc 4, Spring 1980
"The Observatory," Roo Borson

Arc 5, Autumn 1980
"When I Was Fifteen," John Barton
"Poem for Piano and Violin," Don Domanski

Arc 6, Spring 1981
"Other/Mother," Penn Kemp

Arc 7, Autumn 1981
"Treatment" and "Sorceress," Bronwen Wallace

Arc 8/9, Spring/Autumn 1982
"Oranges,"Susan Glickman
"By Thy Senses Sent Forth," Claire Harris
"Getting Born" and "The End of the War," Carol Shields
"Here the Waiting Begins," David Zieroth

Arc 10, Spring 1983
"Summer 1928," Anne Szumigalski

Arc 11, Autumn 1983
"Lost Sisters," Don McKay

Arc 14, Spring 1985
"On the Question of Lisa's Thighs'" Pier Gorgio di Cicco

Arc 15, Autumn 1985

"Beehive Huts." David Manicom

Arc 16, Spring 1986

"Dead Angels," Chirstopher Wiseman

Arc 17, Autumn 1986

"Weird Genes," Patricia Young

Arc 19, Autumn 1987

"Spectacles," Barbara Carey
"The Recalled Hours," Lala Heine-Koehn

Arc 20, Spring 1988

"The Arsonist," Richard Lemm
"Reliquary," Nadine McInnis
"Bone Poems" Don McKay

Arc 22, Spring 1989

"On Rereading *War and Peace* Twenty-three Years Later," Pat Jasper

Arc 23, Autumn 1989

"A Small Earth Trilogy," Di Brandt
"Ceremony for Ancesters: Kōya San," Steven Heighton
"Boy in a Choir," Robert Hilles
"Jesus," Anne Szumigalski

Arc 24, Spring 1990

"Into the Gathering Dark," Jan Conn

Arc 25, Autumn 1990

"The Sparrow Drawer," Diana Brebner
"I Send My Birds Out," Bill Gaston
"Hind, Eating Fish in Denmark," Heather Spears

Arc 26, Spring 1991

"Bloom, Rain," Elisabeth Harvor
"The Health of Poetry," Erin Mouré
"Fedora," Kenneth Sherman

Arc 27, Autumn 1991

"Museum Radiance" Brian Bartlett

Arc 28, Spring 1992

"There Are Charms for Every Kind of Journey," Karen Connelly
"Green as the Vein in a Young Man's Desire... Eastwood 1906,"
Barry Dempster
"Snow Music," Robin Skelton

Arc 29, Autumn 1992

"Woman with Suitcase," Brian Henderson
"Their Futures Drift Like Ash Across the City," Sue Wheeler

Arc 30, Spring 1993

"Our Photos of the Children," Don Coles
"Skin Divers," Anne Michaels

Arc 31, Autumn 1993

"Woman with the Flow of Blood," April Bulmer
"Ski Hill," Michael Crummey
"The Tree in the World," Neile Graham
"A Woman is Drawing Her Mother," Sharon Hawkins

Arc 32, Spring 1994

"Travelling Alone," Blaine Marchand
"Shorts Lines" and "Bus Lines," Daniel David Moses
"Leaving the Air," Ellizabeth Philips

Arc 33, Autumn 1994

"Sturgeon," Tim Bowling
"Unconditional Love," Barry Dempster
"blurred buffalo" Carol Malyon

Arc 34, Spring 1995

"Yvette, Yvonne." Jill Battson
"Virginia Woolf's Mother in the Blurred Garden," Stephanie Bolster
"Crown of Roses," Mary di Michele
"tear water pooling" Barbara Folkart

Arc 35, Autumn 1995

"Winged Fish," Gonzalo Millán
"Woman Under the Lindens." Ludwig Zeller

Arc 37, Autumn 1996

"Circumstantial evidence of the Visitation of angels," Roger Nash

Arc 38, Spring 1997

"He Is," Gregory Scofield

Acknowledgements

"Museum Radiance" appeared in *Underwater Carpentry* by Brian Bartlett (Fredericton: Goose Lane Editions, 1993). Reprinted by permission of the author and the publisher; "When I Was Fifteen" appeared in *A Poor Photographer* by John Barton (Victoria: Sono Nis Press, 1981). Reprinted by permission of the author and the publisher; "Yvette, Yvonne" by Jill Battson is reprinted by permission of the author; "vulture" by E. D. Blodgett is reprinted by permission of the author; "Virginia Woolf's Mother in the Blurred Garden" by Stephanie Bolster is reprinted by permission of the author; "The Observatory" by Roo Borson is reprinted by permission of the author; "Sturgeon" appeared in *Low Water Slack* by Tim Bowling (Madeira Park: Nightwood Editons, 1996). Reprinted by permission of the author and the publisher; "A Small Earth Trilogy" appeared in *Agnes in the Sky* by Di Brandt (Winnipeg: Turnstone Press, 1990). Reprinted by permission of the author and the publisher; "The Sparrow Drawer" appared in *Radiant Life Forms* by Diana Brebner (Windsor: Netherlandic Press, 1990). Reprinted by permission of the author and the publisher; "Woman with a Flow of Blood" by April Bulmer is reprinted by permission of the author; "Spectacles" by Barbara Carey is reprinted by permission of the author; "Our Photos of the Children" by Don Coles is reprinted by permission of the author; "Into the Gathering Dark" appeared in *South of the Tudo Bem Café* by Jan Conn (Montreal: Véhicule Press, 1990). Reprinted by permission of the author and the publisher; "There Are Charms for Every Kind of Journey" appeared in *The Disorder of Love* by Karen Connelly (Toronto: Gutter Press, 1997). Reprinted by permission of the author and the publisher; "Ski Hill" appeared in *Arguments with Gravity* by Michael Crummey (Kingston: Quarry Press, 1996). Reprinted by permission of the author and the publisher; "Green as a the Vein in a Young Man's Desire" appeared in *Letters from a Long Illness with the World: The D. H. Lawrence Poems* by Barry Dempster (London: Brick Books, 1993). Reprinted by permission of the author and the publisher; "Unconditional Love" appeared in *Fire and Brimstone* by Barry Dempster (Montreal: Empyreal Press, 1998). Reprinted by permission of the author and the publisher; "On the Question of Lisa's Thighs" by Pier Giorgio di Cicco is reprinted by permission of the author; Excerpts from "Crown of Roses" appeared in *Debriefing the Rose* by Mary di Michelle (Concord: House of Anansi Press, 1998). Reprinted by permission of the author and the publisher; "Poem for Piano and Violin" appeared in *War in an Empty House* by Don Domanski (Toronto: House of Anansi Press, 1982. Reprinted by permission of the author and the publisher; "tear water dreaming" by Barbara Folkart is reprinted by permission of the author; "I Send My Birds Out" appeared in *Inviting Blindness* by Bill Gaston (Lantzville: Oolichan Books, 1995). Reprinted by permission of the author and the publisher; "Oranges" by Susan Glickman is reprinted by

permission of the author; "The Tree in the World" by Neile Graham is
reprinted by permission of the author; "By Thy Senses Sent Forth"
appeared in *Travelling to Find a Remedy* by Claire Harris (Fredericton:
Goose Lane Editions, 1984). Reprinted by permission of the author and
the publisher; "Bloom, Rain" appeared in *Fortress of Chairs* by Elisabeth
Harvor (Montreal: Véhicule Press, 1992). Reprinted by permission of the
author and the publisher; "A Woman is Drawing Her Mother" by Sharon
Hawkins is reprinted by permission of the author; "Ceremony for
Ancestors: Kōya-San" by Steven Heighton is reprinted by permission of
the author; "The Recalled Hours" by Lala Heine-Koehn is reprinted by
permission of the author; "Woman with Suitcase" by David Henderson is
reprinted by permission of the author; "Boy in a Choir" appeared in
Finding the Lights On by Robert Hilles (Don Mills: Wolsak and Wynn,
1991). Reprinted by permission of the author and the publisher; "On
Reading *War and Peace* Twenty-Three Years Later" appeared in *The
Outlines of Our Warm Bodies* by Pat Jasper (Fredericton: Goose Lane
Editons, 1990). Reprinted by permission of the author and the publisher;
"Other/Mother" by Penn Kemp is reprinted by permission of the author;
"The Arsonist" by Richard Lemm is reprinted by permission of the author;
"blurred buffalo" by Carol Malyon is reprinted by permission of the author;
"Beehive Huts" by David Manicom is reprinted by permission of the
author; "Travelling Alone" appeared in *Bodily Presence* by Blaine Marchand
(Kingston: Quarry Press, 1995). Reprinted by permission of the author and
the publisher; "Reliquary" appeared in *The Litmus Body* by Nadine
McInnis (Kingston: Quarry Press, 1992). Reprinted by permission of the
author and the publisher; "Lost Sisters" appeared in *Sanding Down This
Rocking Chair on a Windy Night* by Don McKay (Toronto: McClelland &
Stewart, 1987) and "Bone Poems" in *Night Field* by Don McKay (Toronto:
McClelland & Stewart, 1991). Reprinted by permission of the author and
the publisher; "Still Life" by Florence McNeil is reprinted by permission
of the author; "Skin Divers" by Anne Michaels is reprinted by permission
of the author; "Winged Fish" by Gonzalo Millán appeared in *Strange
Houses: Selected Poems* by Gonzalo Millán; translated by Annegrit Nill
(Ottawa: Split Quotation, 1991) Reprinted by permission of the author and
the publisher; "Shorts Lines" and "Bus Lines" by Daniel David Moses is
reprinted by permission of the author; "The Health of Poetry" appeared in
Sheepish Beauty, Civilian Love by Erin Mouré (Montreal: Véhicule Press,
1992). Reprinted by permission of the author and the publisher;
"Circumstantial evidence of the visitation of angels" appeared in *In the
Kosher Chow Mein Restaurant* by Roger Nash (Sudbury: Your Scrivener
Press, 1996). Reprinted by permission of the author and the publisher;
"Leaving the Air" appeared in *Beyond My Keeping* by Elizabeth Philips
(Regina: Coteau Books, 1995. Reprinted by permission of the author and
the publisher; "He Is" appeared in *Sâkihtowin-Maskihkiy Êkwa Pêyak
Nikamowin (Love Medicine and One Song)* by Gregory Scofield (Victoria:
Polestar Book Publishers, 1997). Reprinted by permission of the author

and the publisher; "Getting Born" and "The End of the War" appeared in *Coming to Canada* by Carol Shields (Ottawa: Carleton University Press, 1992). Reprinted by permission of the author and the publisher; "Fedora: A Child's Song" appeared in *Open to Currents* by Kenneth Sherman (Don Mills: Wolsak and Wynn, 1992). Reprinted by permission of the author and the publisher; "Snow Music" appeared in *Popping Fuchsias* by Robin Skelton (Vancouver: Ronsdale Press, 199). Reprinted by permission of Sylvia Skelton and the publisher; "Hind, Eating Fish in Denmark" appeared in *Human Acts* by Heather Spears (Don Mills: Wolsak and Wynn, 1991). Reprinted by permission of the author and the publisher; "Running in Darkness" by Peter Stevens is reprinted by permission of the author; "Jesus" appeared in *Rapture of the Deep* (Regina: Coteau Books, 1991) and "Summer 1928" in *On Glassy Wings: Poems New and Selected* (Coteau Books, 1997) by Anne Szumigalski. Reprinted by permission of the author and the publisher; "Sorceress" and "Treatment" appeared in *Signs of the Former Tenant* by Bronwen Wallace (Ottawa: Oberon, 1983). Reprinted by permission of The Estate of Bronwen Wallace and the publisher; "Their Futures Drift Like Ash Across the City" appeared in *Solstice on the Anacortes Ferry* (Vernon: Kalamalka Press, 1995). Reprinted by permission of the author and the publisher; "Dead Angels" appeared in *Postcards Home: Poems New and Selected* by Christopher Wiseman (Sono Nis Press, 1988). Reprinted by permission of the author and the publisher; "Weird Genes" by Patricia Young is reprinted by permission of the author; "Woman Under the Lindens" appeared in *Body of Insomnia and Other Poems* by Ludwig Zeller; translated by A. F. Moritz and Teresa Moritz (Victoria: Ekstasis Editions, 1996). Reprinted by permission of the author, the translators and the publisher; "Here the Waiting Begins" appeared in *When the Stones Fly Up* by David Zieroth (Toronto: House of Anansi Press, 1985). Reprinted by permission of the author and the publisher.

Contributors

Brian Bartlett of Halifax has published several books of poetry, most recently, *Granite Erratics* (Ekstasis, 1997). He has won a Hawthornden Fellowship and two *Malahat Review* Long Poem Prizes.

John Barton has published seven collections of award-winning poetry, including *Notes Toward a Family Tree*, *Designs from the Interior* and most recently, *Sweet Ellipsis*, published by ECW in spring 1998.

Jill Battson is an internationally published poet and performer living in Toronto. Her latest book is *Hard Candy*, published by Insomniac Press.

E.D. Blodgett is University Professor of Comparative Literature at the University of Alberta where he remains happily devoted to his muse.

Stephanie Bolster's *White Stone: the Alice Poems* recently appeared from Véhicule Press. The winner of the Bronwen Wallace Award (1996) and *The Malahat Review* Long Poem Prize (1997), she lives in Ottawa.

Roo Borson's most recent collections are *Nightwalk, Selected Poems* (Oxford University Press, 1994) and *Water Memory* (McClelland & Stewart).

Tim Bowling is the author of two volumes: *Low Water Slack* (Nightwood, 1995) and *Dying Scarlet* (Nightwood, 1997). A native of Vancouver and Ladner, B.C., he currently lives in Edmonton.

Di Brandt teaches English and Creative Writing at the University of Windsor, and is a former poetry editor of *Prairie Fire*. She has won numerous awards for her poetry.

Diana Brebner has published three books of poetry, *Radiant Life Forms* (1990), *The Golden Lotus* (1993) and *Flora and Fauna* (1996). She is currently working on a new poetry collection, *The Ishtar Gate*.

April Bulmer has published two books of poetry: *The Weight of Wings* (Trout Lily Press, 1997) and *A Salve for Every Sore* (Cormorant Books, 1991). She lives in Cambridge, Ontario.

Barbara Carey is a poet and editor living in Toronto. Her latest book is *The Ground of Events* (Mercury).

Don Coles's *Forests of the Medieval World* won the Governor General's Award in 1993, and *For the Living and the Dead* won the John Glassco Translation Prize in 1997.

Jan Conn is presently an assistant professor in the Department of Biology, University of Vermont. Her most recent book of poetry is *What Dante Did With Loss* (Véhicule, 1994).

Karen Connelly's latest collection of poetry is *The Disorder of Love* (Gutter Press, 1997). She is currently working on a novel about a Burmese political prisoner.

Michael Crummey's first poetry collection, *Arguments With Gravity*, was published by Quarry Press in 1996. A second collection, *Hard Light*, is due from Brick Books in 1998.

Ontario writer Barry Dempster has published ten books including *Letters from a Long Illness with the World*, *Fire and Brimstone* and a novel, *The Ascension of Jesse Rapture*.

Pier Giorgio di Cicco was born in Arezzo, Italy in 1949. His poem was written in the early eighties. He lives on a farm in Nobleton, Ontario "surrounded by friends and many ladybugs".

Mary di Michele teaches English at Concordia University. She is the author of eight volumes of poetry, the most recent, *Debriefing the Rose*, (Anansi, 1998) and one novel, *Under My Skin* (Quarry, 1995).

Don Domanski was born in Sydney, N.S. in 1950 and now lives in Halifax. His most recent book is *Parish of the Physic Moon* (McClelland & Stewart, 1998).

Barbara Folkart "began" in *Arc* 28. She has since published extensively in Canada and the U.K. She will always be grateful for the nurturing of people like Nadine McInnis.

New Brunswick writer Bill Gaston is author of six books of fiction, including *Tall Lives*, *North of Jesus' Beans* and *Fire Heaven*. His poetry collection, *Inviting Blindness*, appeared in 1995.

The version of "Oranges" included here predates that in Susan Glickman's first book, *Complicity* (1983). She has published three other volumes of poetry, and *The Picturesque and the Sublime: A Poetics of the Canadian Landscape*.

A Canadian writer living in Seattle, Neile Graham's work appears in numerous anthologies and magazines. Her most recent collection, *Spells for Clear Vision* (1994), was shortlisted for the Lowther Awards.

Claire Harris' latest book is *Dipped in Shadow*, Goose Lane Editions, 1996. It was shortlisted for the Writer's Guild of Alberta Prize in 1997.

Elisabeth Harvor is the author of three story collections. Her first book of poetry, *Fortress of Chairs*, won the Lampert Award. Her second book, *The Long Cold Green Evenings of Spring*, has just come out with Signal Editions.

Sharon Hawkins is an associate editor of Arc. She is currently preparing her first manuscript, *Preserving Jars*. A poem series will appear in *Quintet* (BuschekBooks), an upcoming collection by women writers.

Steven Heighton won the Gerald Lampert Award for his first poetry collection, *Stalin's Carnival*, and was a Governor General's Award finalist for his most recent collection, *The Ecstasy of Skeptics* (Anansi, 1994).

Lala Heine-Koehn was born in Poland and studied International Law and Voice in Munich. She emigrated to Canada, first to Saskatchewan and then to Victoria. Her seventh book of poetry is coming out in 1998 as well as a whimsical prose collection of fairytales and animal stories.

David Henderson has lived many years in the Ottawa area. His poetry has appeared in the *Antigonish Review*, *Scrivener*, *Vintage 94*, *Whetstone*, *Cumberland Poetry Review* and *Zygote* among others.

Robert Hilles lives in Calgary. Nine of his twelve books are poetry, with *Cantos From A Small Room* winning the 1994 Governor General's Award. His latest collections are *Nothing Vanishes*, and *Breathing Distance*. He is currently writing a novel, *A Gradual Ruin*.

Pat Jasper lives in Etobicoke, Ontario, and has published two collections of poetry: *Recycling* in 1985 and *The Outlines of Our Warm Bodies* in 1990, both from Goose Lane Editions.

Penn Kemp lives in Toronto. Her most recent books include *Some Talk Magic* (1986), *Throo* (1988) and *The Universe is One Poem* (1990).

Richard Lemm has published three collections of poetry. He teaches English and Creative Writing at the University of Prince Edward Island.

Carol Malyon's latest books are a short story collection, *Lovers & Other Strangers*, and a picture book for children, *Mixed-up Grandmas*. She lives in Toronto and was the Fall 1997 writer-in-residence at the University of New Brunswick.

David Manicom's third collection of poetry is *The Older Graces* (Oolichen, 1997). His most recent books are *Ice in Dark Water* (fiction, Véhicule) and *Progeny of Ghosts: Travels in Russia and the Old Empire* (Oolichan, 1998)

Blaine Marchand's fourth book of poetry was *Bodily Presence* (Quarry Press, 1995). He is working on a collection of short fiction entitled *Nomads*. The title story will appear in *Contra/dictions* (Arsenal Press) in Fall 1998.

Don McKay's eight books include *Birding, or desire*, *Night Field* and *Apparatus*. He has taught (UWO, UNB), edited (*The Fiddlehead*, *Brick Books*), co-ordinated workshops and studies (Sagehill, Banff) and received a Governor General's Award in 1991.

Nadine McInnis lives in Ottawa. She has published three books of poetry, *Shaking the Dreamland Tree*, *The Litmus Body*, and *Hand to Hand* (Polestar, 1998) and a critical study of Dorothy Livesay's erotic poetry, *The Poetics of Desire*.

Florence McNeil has published nine books of poetry and edited three. She is the author of a novel, *Breathing Each Other's Air* as well as three young adult novels. She has taught at universities and now writes full time. She lives in Vancouver.

Anne Michaels has published two books of poetry, with a third, *Skin Divers*, forthcoming. She is also the author of the international bestselling novel, *Fugitive Pieces*.

Gonzalo Millán has published five books of poetry in Spanish, four written in Canada. After living in the Netherlands and Canada, he returned to Chile in 1984, where he was awarded the Pablo Neruda Prize.

First Nations writer Daniel David Moses lives in Toronto. His publications include *The Indian Medicine Shows* (Exile), *Delicate Bodies* (Nightwood) and *An Anthology of Canadian Native Literature in English* (Oxford)

Erin Mouré lives in Montreal. Her most recent book is *Search Procedures* (Anansi, 1996).

Roger Nash teaches at Laurentian University. His most recent book of poems is *In the Kosher Chow Mein Restaurant*.

Elizabeth Philips is a poet, editor and journalist. Her most recent collection is *Beyond My Keeping* (Coteau, 1995). She lives in Saskatoon.

Gregory Scofield is a mixed-blood writer/storyteller of Cree, Scottish, English and French ancestry. His third collection, *Sâkihtowin-Maskihkiy Êkwa Pêyak Nikamowin (Love Medicine and One Song)* was published by Polestar.

Kenneth Sherman has published several books of poetry, including *Words for Elephant Man* and *Jackson's Point*. His most recent books are *Clusters* (poems, 1997) and *Void and Voice* (essays, 1998).

Carol Shields lives in Winnipeg. Her most recent books include *Coming to Canada: poems* (1992), *Larry's Party* (1997) and *A Celibate Season* (1998).

Robin Skelton, before he died in Victoria in 1997, published more than 100 books in diverse genres. A native of Yorkshire, during the 1950s he published his early poetry in *The Times Literary Supplement, Outposts, The Listener* and *London Magazine* before emigrating to Canada in 1963. Committed to beginning writers throughout his life, he founded the Department of Writing at the University of Victoria in 1973.

Heather Spears is a Canadian poet, novelist and artist. She has won several awards, including the Governor General's Award for Poetry in 1988 for the collection *The Word for Sand*. She lives in Denmark.

Peter Stevens lives in Windsor, Ontario. His most recent books include *Swimming in the Afternoon: Selected Poems* (1992) and *Thinking into the Dark* (1997).

Anne Szumigalski has lived in Saskatchewan since 1951. Her latest book is *On Glassy Wings, New and Selected Poems* (Coteau, 1997), just won the CAA Award for Poetry.

Bronwen Wallace was the author of five volumes of poetry, one collection of short stories and one collection of journalism. She was a major influence on many writers, both emerging and well-known. She died at the age of 44 in Kingston, where she lived most of her life.

Sue Wheeler lives on Lasquite Island, BC. Her book, *Solstice on the Anacortes Ferry* (Kalamalka, 1995), won the Kalamalka New Writer's Award. "Their Futures..." won the 1992 Gwendolyn MacEwan Memorial Award.

Christopher Wiseman's eighth book of poetry will soon appear from the Porcupine's Quill. He started the creative writing programme at the University of Calgary.

Patricia Young's most recent book, *What I Remember from My Time on Earth* (Anansi, 1997), just won the Dorothy Livesay Award.

Ludwig Zeller lives in Oaxaca, Mexico. His most recent book of poems in English, *Body of Insomnia and Other Poems* (Ekstasis,1996) was translated by A. F. Moritz and Teresa Moritz.

David Zieroth has recently published *How I Joined Humanity at Last* (Harbour, 1998). He teaches at Douglas College in New Westminster, BC where he edited *Event* from 1985 to 1996.